GOAL!

Penguin Random House

Senior editor Chris Hawkes
Senior art editors Mik Gates, Stefan Podhorodecki
Editor Suhel Ahmed
Designers David Ball, Chrissy Barnard,
Kit Lane, Simon Mumford, Sadie Thomas
Illustrations Adam Benton, Stuart Jackson-Carter,
Jon@kja-artists
Creative retouching Steve Crozier
Picture research Nic Dean, Surya Sarangi

Senior jacket designer Mark Cavanagh
Jacket designers Tanya Mehrotra, Suhita Dharamjit
Jacket editor Claire Gell
Jackets editorial coordinator Priyanka Sharma
DTP designer Rakesh Kumar
Managing jackets editor Saloni Singh
Jacket design development manager
Sophia MTT
Consultant Tracey Bourne (Football Studies –
Southampton Solent University; FA Associate tutor)
Producer (pre-production) Jacqueline Street
Senior producer Gary Batchelor

Managing art editor Philip Letsu
Managing editor Francesca Baines
Publisher Andrew Macintyre
Art director Karen Self
Associate publishing director Liz Wheeler
Publishing director Jonathan Metcalf

First published in Great Britain in 2017
by Dorling Kindersley Limited
80 Strand, London, WC2R 0RL

A CIP catalogue record for this book
is available from the British Library.

ISBN: 978-1-4654-6364-7

Printed and bound in China

Discover more at
www.dk.com

CONTENTS

The beautiful game

Play to the whistle

A team game

Tournaments and trophies

Individual skills

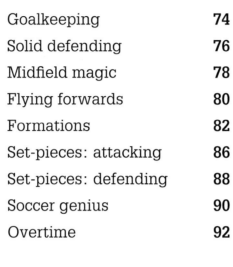

Club world

The beautiful game

No one knows who invented soccer. However, once the game's rules were set down, in 1863, it did not take long for soccer to reach every corner of the world. Today, it is the most popular sport on the planet, with around 3.5 billion fans.

Ancient ball games

Humans have been playing ball games **for at least 4,000 years**. Each of these early games had their **own rules**, some of which are **similar to soccer**.

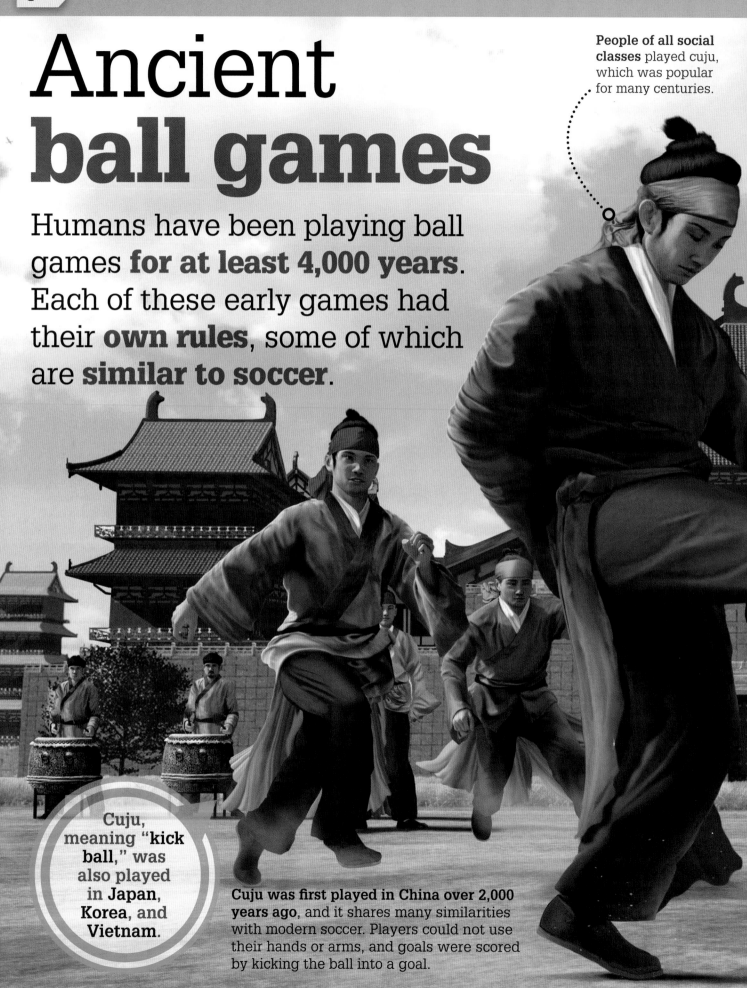

People of all social **classes** played cuju, which was popular for many centuries.

Cuju, meaning **"kick ball,"** was also played in **Japan, Korea,** and **Vietnam**.

Cuju was first played in China over 2,000 years ago, and it shares many similarities with modern soccer. Players could not use their hands or arms, and goals were scored by kicking the ball into a goal.

MESOAMERICAN BALL GAME

Played in Central America 3,600 years ago, the Meso-american ball game is the world's oldest team sport. Players played on a court, could not use their hands, and scored goals by getting the ball to go through a hoop.

A competitive game consisted of two teams of 12–16 players on each side.

Individual players attracted fame and fortune, and, by the 10th century, there was even a national championship to decide the best team.

The ball had an outer covering made of leather and was stuffed tightly with feathers.

Birth of soccer

A variety of soccerlike games were played in **English boarding schools** in the **mid-19th century**. However, **the rules** of these games were **so different**, that it was virtually impossible for the school teams to play against each other.

Eight players make up the bully: three "corners," 2 "sideposts," one "post," one "pup," and one "fly."

Players outside the bully are called "behinds." Their role is to kick the ball over the bully toward the opponent's goal.

Behinds are made up of two types of player: "shorts" and "longs."

> The rules for the **Eton Field Game** were first written down in 1815.

THE FOOTBALL ASSOCIATION (FA)

Englishman Ebenezer Morley could be called the father of the Football Association. His letter, suggesting that soccer should have a common set of rules (meaning that teams could play against each other), led to a series of meetings that ended with the foundation of the Football Asssociation on October 26, 1863. The game's first set of rules were published a few months later.

At the school of Eton, they played—and still do—the "Field Game." As in soccer, the ball is round and players are not allowed to pick up. However, the rules are more complicated than in soccer, and there is also a scrum, called a "bully."

FIRST INTERNATIONAL

The first international was played between England and Scotland in Glasgow, Scotland, in 1872. It finished 0–0.

Soccer spread to countries through the many connections of the British Empire, introduced by the huge number of British workers who traveled throughout the world. It did not take long before these countries started to form their own national associations.

1863 The Football Association, soccer's first national governing body, is established in England.

1876 The Welsh FA is founded.

1891 New Zealand becomes the first country outside Europe to create a national association.

1893 The first national association in South America is established in Argentina.

1904 The Haiti Football association is formed—the first in North America.

1921 Egypt becomes the first African country to create a national association.

1924 The Chinese Football Association is founded.

1928 Israel and Palestine both create national associations.

1860

1873 Scotland forms the world's second national association.

1890

1889 Denmark and the Netherlands become the first countries on continental Europe to create national associations.

1912 The Canadian Soccer Association is founded. The US Soccer Federation follows a year later.

1920

1939 By the start of World War II, there were 109 national associations.

Soccer spreads around the world

Established in 1857, **Sheffield FC** is the **world's** oldest soccer club.

After the Football Assocation was established in England in 1863, it took **little more than a century** for soccer to appear in **every continent** and **virtually every country** in the world.

1947 A national association is created in newly formed Pakistan.

1965 The Zimbabwe Football Association is formed after the country gains its independence from Britain.

1971 The United Arab Emirates Football Association is formed in the same year the country is created.

1989 Belarus becomes the first former Soviet state to form its own national association.

2011 South Sudan becomes the latest country to form a national association.

1950

1980

2010

1960 Twelve national associations are formed around the world; the most in a single year.

1961 Football Federation Australia is formed, 70 years after its equivalent in New Zealand.

1991 The South African Football Association is reformed following the end of apartheid.

The modern era

The **Fédération Internationale de Football Association (FIFA)** is the game's international governing body. **Every continent**, with the exception of Antarctica, **has its own confederation**, which organizes international and club competitions.

CONCACAF

CONCACAF governs the game in North and Central America and the Caribbean. Its headquarters are in New York, NY.

Formed: 1961
Members: 41
Major tournaments:
International:
CONCACAF Gold Cup
Club: CONCACAF Champions League

UEFA

UEFA is the governing body of soccer in Europe. Its headquarters are located in Nyon, Switzerland.

Formed: 1954
Members: 55
Major tournaments:
International:
UEFA European
Championship;

Club: UEFA Champions League,
UEFA Europa League

CONMEBOL

The oldest of the continental confederations, CONMEBOL was formed in 1916. It governs soccer in South America and its headquarters are in Luque, Paraguay.

Formed: 1916
Members: 10
Major tournaments:
International: Copa América
Club: Copa Libertadores, Copa Sudamericana

CAF

The CAF governs soccer in Africa and has more members than the other confederations. Its headquarters are in Cairo, Egypt.

Formed: 1957
Members: 56
Major tournaments:
International: Africa Cup of Nations
Club: CAF Champions League, CAF Confederation Cup

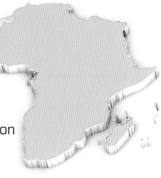

FIFA

FIFA is soccer's global governing body and organizes the game's major international tournaments. Its headquarters are in Zurich, Switzerland.

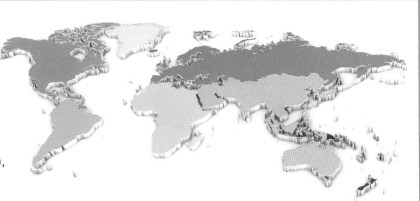

Formed: 1904
Members: 211
Major tournaments:
FIFA World Cup, FIFA Women's World Cup, FIFA Confederations Cup, Olympic Games

AFC

The AFC governs soccer in Asia and, since 2006, Australia, from its headquarters in Kuala Lumpur, Malaysia.

Formed: 1954
Members: 47
Major tournaments:
International:
AFC Asia Cup
Club: AFC Champions League, AFC Cup

FIFA's motto is: "For the game. For the world."

OFC

Founded in 1966, the OFC is the youngest of soccer's confederations. It governs the game in Oceania from its headquarters in Auckland, New Zealand.

Formed: 1966
Members: 14
Major tournaments:
International:
OFC Nations Cup
Club: Oceania Club Championship

CUT OFF IN ITS PRIME

By 1920, the women's game was as popular as the men's, with one game in England featuring Dick, Kerr's Ladies (above, right), attracting a crowd of 53,000. In 1921, however, the FA banned women's games at their fields, saying the sport was inappropriate for women.

1881 An unofficial women's international game is played between Scotland and England in Edinburgh on May 7, 1881. Scotland win 3–0.

1921 The Football Association bans women's teams from playing on association member's fields.

1890s Several women's clubs are formed in England. One game, in north London, attracted a crowd of 10,000.

1930s Women's leagues are established in France and Italy.

1881

1930

1919 The first-ever women's French Championship is played—only two teams take part.

1920 Dick, Kerr's Ladies, England's leading women's team, play a French XI in France. They win the game 2–0, in front of a crowd of 62,000.

Women's soccer

Action from the 2015 FIFA Women's World Cup game between the Ivory Coast and Thailand (which Thailand won 3–2). The tournament, held in Canada, featured 24 teams for the first time and was shown on television in 171 countries.

Women's soccer has gone through many **ups and downs** over the years. Once as popular as the men's game, it was then **banned**, but it has enjoyed a **huge resurgence** in recent times.

1951 The first women's league is established in the United States.

1971 The FA lifts its ban on women's soccer. The same year, UEFA recommends the women's game should be taken under the control of the national associations of each country.

1984 Sweden wins the first official UEFA Women's European Championship.

1996 Women's soccer is included in the program of events at the Olympic Games for the first time.

2017 The number of national women's teams participating in international games rises to 176.

1960

1980

1969 A group of women's clubs form the Women's FA in England.

1989 Japan becomes the first country to launch a semi-professional women's league.

1991 The United States wins the first FIFA Women's World Cup.

1957 Germany organizes an unofficial women's European Championship.

The first **FIFA-approved women's international** was played in **1971**.

Overtime

The **10 essentials** of the ancient Chinese game of **cuju** included: respect for other players, courtesy, *team spirit*, no ungentlemanly behavior, no dangerous play, **and no ball-hogging.**

Balls in the **Mesoamerican ball game** from Central America varied; some were as small as **tennis balls**, while others could weigh up to 8 lb (3.6 kg)—that's the same weight as a **watermelon**.

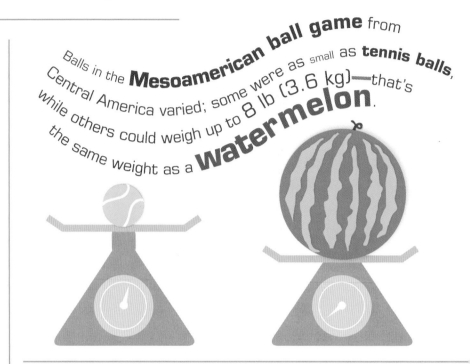

80 percent of FIFA member associations have a **senior women's team.**

1,166,926 girls around the world play in grassroots soccer programs.

Countries with the most registered players

If a player plays for a club, they are normally registered with their national football or soccer association. The graphic below shows the countries with the most registered players (female and male).

United States 1 — 1.6 million
Germany 2 — 871,000
Canada 3 — 495,000

Germany 1 — 5.4 million
United States 2 — 2.5 million
Brazil 3 — 2.1 million

Female players

Male players

The world's richest leagues

Football leagues make the majority of their money by selling the rights to show games to television companies. The world's top-five richest leagues are all in Europe, with England's Premier League at the top.

Premier League England
$ 4.5 billion

Bundesliga Germany
$ 3.6 billion

Ligue 1 France
$ 1.5 billion

Serie A Italy
$ 2 billion

La Liga Spain
$ 2.7 billion

50 percent

of FIFA member association countries have a **youth team**.

Countries with the most players

In 2007, FIFA conducted a survey to find out which countries had the most soccer players (registered and unregistered). Here are the top eight.

FIFA **has 211 members**, **compared with the** United Nation's **193**.

China
26.1 million

United States
24.4 million

India
20.5 million

Germany
16.3 million

Mexico
8.4 million

Indoneisia
7.1 million

Nigeria
6.7 million

Brazil
13.1 million

Play to the whistle

Anyone can play soccer: all you need is a ball and a space to play. Even the professional game is relatively simple: two teams of 11 players play for 90 minutes, while three game officials (the referee and the assistant referees) ensure that both teams play to the Laws of the Game.

Laws of the game

Soccer has **17 laws** that cover every aspect of the game. The **English FA** devised 13 of these in **1863**. The remaining four were added later on.

5 **The referee**
The appointed referee, whose decisions are final, is in charge of the game.

6 **Assistant referees**
Two officials are appointed to support the referee to enforce the rules.

7 **Game duration**
A game is played over two periods of 45 minutes each.

5. The referee

1 **Field of play**
The field size may vary, but must be rectangle, with the correct markings.

1. Field of play

1863   1891   1902

2 **The ball**
The ball must weigh 14–16 oz (400–450 g) and be about 8.65 in (22 cm) across.

3 **Number of players**
A team has 11 players. A game cannot take place with fewer than seven players in a team.

3. Number of players

4 **Players' equipment**
Players must wear a jersey, shorts, socks, shin guards, and soccer cleats.

The original "Laws of the Game" were handwritten by Ebenezer Cobb Morley in 1863.

8 **Start/restart of play**
A kick off starts play, and restarts the game after a goal.

9 **Ball in play**
The ball is always in play unless the referee stops the game.

10 **Method of scoring**
A goal is scored when the whole ball crosses the line of the goal.

11 **Offside**
A player is offside if he or she goes behind the line of opposing defenders before receiving the ball from a teammate.

12 **Fouls and misconduct**
Players must play the game fairly and safely, and will be penalized for any unfair or unsporting behavior.

13 **Free kick**
A team wins a free kick for any foul or offense committed against them. It is taken from the spot where the offense occurred.

14 **Penalty kick**
A team wins a penalty kick for any foul committed by an opponent in the opposition's own penalty area.

15 **Throw-in**
A team wins a throw-in when the ball crosses the touchline after touching an opposition player last.

16 **Goal kick**
The defending team wins a goal kick if the ball crosses their own goal line after touching an opposition player last.

17 **Corner kick**
The attacking team wins a corner if an opposition player touches the ball last before it crosses the goal line.

12. Fouls and misconduct

10. Method of scoring

15. Throw-in

17. Corner kick

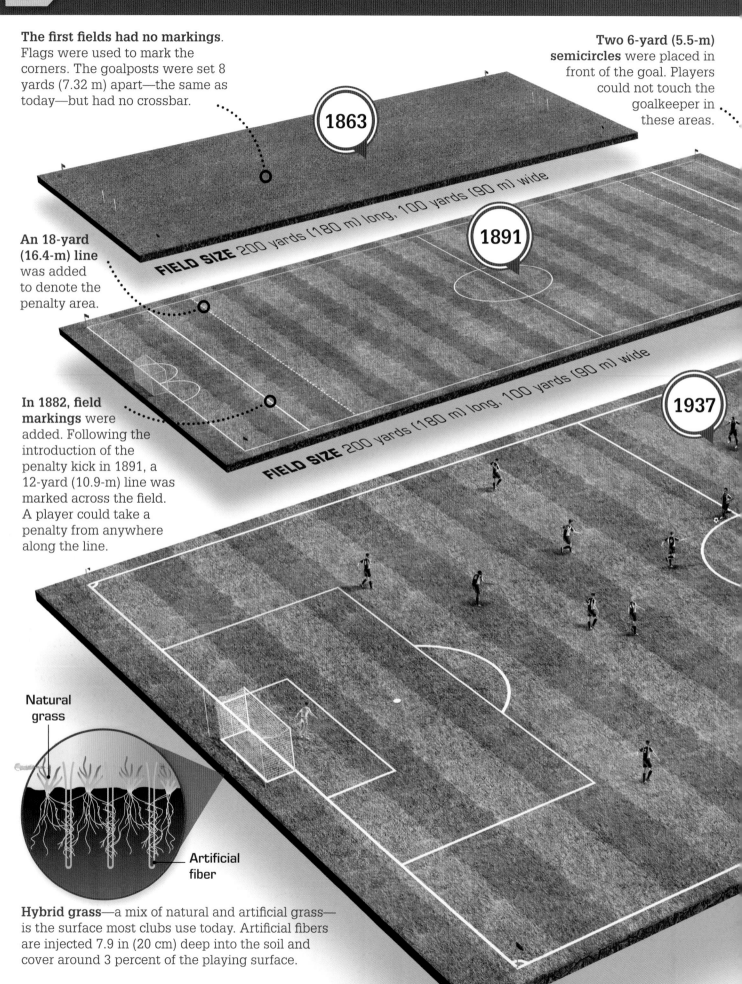

The first fields had no markings. Flags were used to mark the corners. The goalposts were set 8 yards (7.32 m) apart—the same as today—but had no crossbar.

Two 6-yard (5.5-m) semicircles were placed in front of the goal. Players could not touch the goalkeeper in these areas.

1863

FIELD SIZE 200 yards (180 m) long, 100 yards (90 m) wide

1891

An 18-yard (16.4-m) line was added to denote the penalty area.

In 1882, field markings were added. Following the introduction of the penalty kick in 1891, a 12-yard (10.9-m) line was marked across the field. A player could take a penalty from anywhere along the line.

FIELD SIZE 200 yards (180 m) long, 100 yards (90 m) wide

1937

Natural grass

Artificial fiber

Hybrid grass—a mix of natural and artificial grass—is the surface most clubs use today. Artificial fibers are injected 7.9 in (20 cm) deep into the soil and cover around 3 percent of the playing surface.

The field

The FA's first rulebook contained no guidelines for **field markings**, and it was only in the early **20th century** that soccer fields began to take their **modern form**.

A tape was first hung between the goalposts in 1872. It was positioned 8 ft (2.4 m) above the ground. A solid crossbar replaced it in 1875.

The 18-yard (16.4-m) line was shrunk in 1902 to become the penalty area. The D, or arc, of the penalty area was added in 1937 to ensure that players were at least 10 yards (9 m) from the penalty spot when a player took a penalty.

FIELD SIZE 100–120 yards (90–120 m) long, 50–100 yards (45–90 m) wide

The **average field contains** an average of **300 million blades of grass.**

The size and appearance of a soccer field have changed dramatically since the game was first played in 1863. The illustrations above show how field markings have changed over the years.

UNDER-SOIL HEATING

Most clubs have under-soil heating systems beneath the playing surface. These consist of hundreds of yards of tubes that contain hot water pipes that prevent the field from freezing over during winter.

The soccer ball

The **earliest soccer balls** were **inflated pig bladders** covered with leather. Ball technology has changed dramatically over the years, both in terms of **how balls are manufactured** and **what they are made of**.

Medieval soccer players used a leather ball stuffed with an inflated pig's bladder, but this did not bounce well and often deflated. The modern ball has an outer cover made of synthetic leather, an inner lining to make it bouncy, and an inflated rubber bladder in the center.

The oldest-known soccer ball was found in a Scottish castle. When analyzed, it dated back to the 1540s.

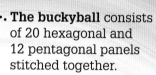

1970s "Buckyball"

1990s ball

1880s ball

The buckyball consists of 20 hexagonal and 12 pentagonal panels stitched together.

1850s ball

Oldest-known soccer ball

FAST FACTS

Soccer balls come in a range of standard sizes depending on the type of soccer being played and the age of the players.

Age: 14+

Size 5 ball
27–28 in
(68.5–71 cm)

Age: Under 14

Size 4 ball
25–26 in
(63.5–66 cm)

Age: Under 9

Size 3 ball
23–24 in
(58.5–61 cm)

Beach soccer ball
27–28 in
(68.5–71 cm)

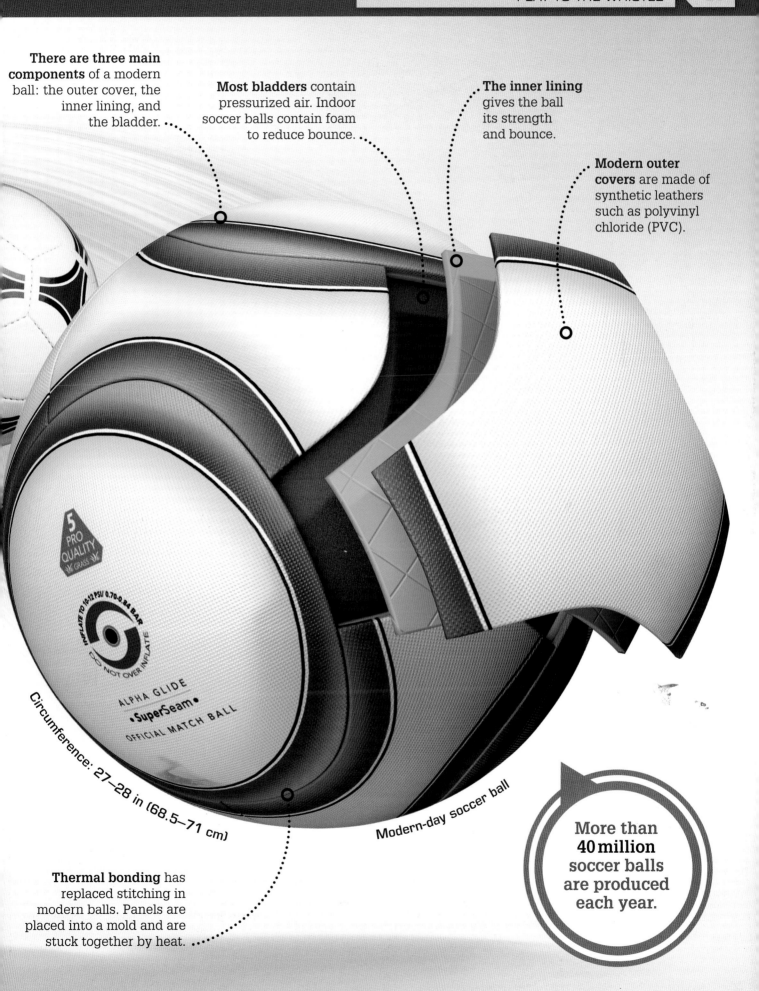

There are three main components of a modern ball: the outer cover, the inner lining, and the bladder.

Most bladders contain pressurized air. Indoor soccer balls contain foam to reduce bounce.

The inner lining gives the ball its strength and bounce.

Modern outer covers are made of synthetic leathers such as polyvinyl chloride (PVC).

5 PRO QUALITY GRASS

INFLATE TO 10-12 PSI/ 0.70-0.84 BAR
DO NOT OVER INFLATE

ALPHA GLIDE
•SuperSeam•
OFFICIAL MATCH BALL

Circumference: 27–28 in (68.5–71 cm)

Modern-day soccer ball

Thermal bonding has replaced stitching in modern balls. Panels are placed into a mold and are stuck together by heat.

More than **40 million** soccer balls are produced each year.

Kitted out

Soccer kits have changed dramatically over the years, from the **thick cotton shirts and baggy shorts** of the 19th century, to the **high tech materials used** to make today's kits.

In 1921, the law was changed so that, in the event of a color clash, the away team (and not the home team) had to change. Nowadays, all teams have a home kit and an away kit, with some teams also having a third kit.

Modern shirts are normally made of a polyester mesh that does not trap in heat or sweat. They also contain lycra, which adds strength and flexibility.

Sleeves can either be long or short according to the Laws of the Game.

Soccer kits are used to distinguish between the two teams when they are on the field. Their design has changed hugely over the years. This illustration compares a kit from the 1890s to that worn by players today.

Early soccer shirts were made of thick cotton and had collars. Some team's shirts were even made of wool!

Team kits started to emerge in the 1870s.

Modern shorts are loose, which allows for freedom of movement and good air circulation.

Future shirts could contain computers that monitor a player's heart rate.

Modern shin pads are made of many different synthetic materials. They are designed to spread the load of any impact over as wide an area as possible.

Socks must entirely cover the shin guard.

Today

1890

Shorts had to cover the knees according to a Football Association rule passed in 1904.

The first player to wear shin guards was Nottingham Forest's Sam Weller Widdowson in 1874. He wore a pair of cut-down cricket pads strapped to the outside of his socks.

Socks worn by early players could be any color. Clubs were not required to register the color and design of their socks until 1937.

Perfect cleats

Early soccer cleats were designed to provide players with **both protection** and **grip on the field**. Nowadays, following years of development, the main function of the modern cleat is to **improve a player's performance**.

The cleat's surface contains ridges of varying sizes. These are designed to aid touch and ball control.

The upper part of the cleat is flexible, which helps the player's movement.

Studs have been shaped like arrows. Tests show that this shape provides better grip.

Modern cleats are a product of detailed research into comfort, a player's movement, and which part of the foot comes into contact with the ball the most.

An elasticated, knitted collar aids movement, ensures the cleat is more firmly attached to the foot, and is comfortable.

EARLY CLEATS

Early soccer cleats were made of leather, were uncomfortable, and heavy. It was not until 1891 that the Football Association allowed cleats to be fitted with studs.

The cleat's sole is shaped to fit the foot perfectly.

The earliest-known soccer cleats were worn by English king Henry VIII in 1526.

The cleat's plastic sole is flexible to increase a player's mobility.

The position of the studs has been established after detailed research into a player's movement on the field.

Top-flight referees carry hi-tech equipment worth up to $4,500 onto the field. The figure excludes the Goal line Technology system, which costs about $650,000 to install in the stadium.

A headset is used by the referee to communicate with the assistant referees. It is designed to ensure that they can hear one another clearly—even inside a noisy stadium.

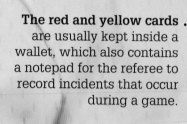

The red and yellow cards are usually kept inside a wallet, which also contains a notepad for the referee to record incidents that occur during a game.

A two-way radio receiver relays the messages from the headset. The radio is powered by a battery pack.

Before whistles, referees used **handkerchiefs** to draw the attention of players.

The Goal line Technology (GLT) wrist device is linked to a computerized camera system, which monitors both goals, and alerts the referee if the ball fully crosses either goal line.

The referee

The referee is responsible for **enforcing** the **Laws of the Game**. At elite level, referees are equipped with **state-of-the-art technology** to help them with their job.

The signal beep system buzzes and vibrates whenever either assistant referee presses a button on their flags. This alerts the referee to any infringement.

A stopwatch is used to keep track of the game time. At elite level, the watch also includes a heart rate monitor to measure the referee's fitness level.

MARKER SPRAYS

When a team is awarded a free kick, the referee uses a foaming spray to create a temporary marker 10 yards (9.1 m) away from the kick. The defenders must stand behind the mark at the moment the free kick is taken.

A whistle is used to signal the start and restart the game, stop play due to a foul or injury, and to end each half.

Assistant referees

Assistant referees help the referee enforce the **Laws of the Game.**

One assistant referee runs along each touchline and is responsible for one half of the field. The **referee may overrule** any decisions made by an assistant referee.

An **assistant referee communicates** with the referee via a small radio set.

Assistant referees officiate in situations in which the referee is not ideally positioned to see an incident and make the best decision.

A **button on the flag** to alert the referee instantly of any decision. This sends a beeping or vibrating signal to the referee.

Assistant referees were **known as linesmen** before 1996.

The flag is brightly colored to ensure that it draws the referee's attention when the assistant referee makes a signal.

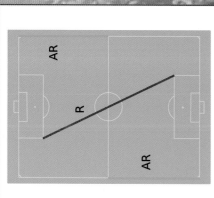

FAST FACTS

The Diagonal System
is the most common method used by referees to officiate in a game. The referee (R) patrols a diagonal line that runs from the opposite corners of each penalty area. Each assistant referee (AR) is responsible for a separate half of the field.

Assistant referees use a set of standard flag signals to alert the referee to incidents and infringements that occur in their half of the field.

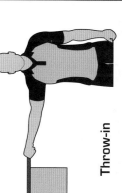

Substitution

A flag is held above the head with both hands to indicate a team's wish to make a substitution.

Offside

The flag is held above the head to signal for an offside offense.

Throw-in

A flag is held out to one side, pointing in the direction of play of the team awarded the throw-in.

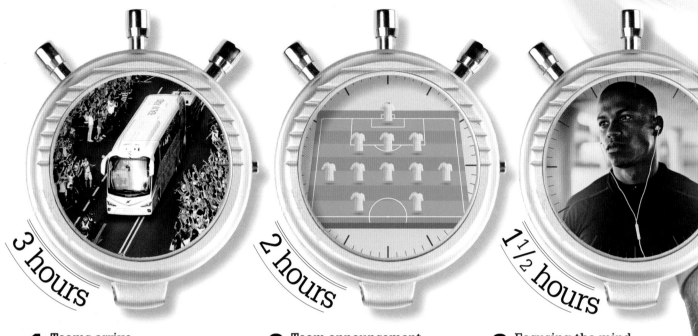

3 hours

2 hours

1½ hours

1 **Teams arrive**
Players make their way to the stadium up to three hours before kick off. The away team arrives on the team bus.

2 **Team announcement**
Both managers reveal their team's starting line up and the list of substitutes to the press.

3 **Focusing the mind**
Players begin their mental preparation. They each have their own ritual for staying relaxed and focused right up to kick off.

In 2012, GSP Polet's Vuk Bakic scored **directly from a kick off** in a Serbian league game.

Countdown to **kick off**

Before the **game** kicks off, the players spend up to **two hours** preparing for the **physical** and **mental** challenges of the game ahead.

15 mins

15 mins

5 mins

4 Warm-up
Players take part in low-level exercise drills to warm up key muscle groups.

5 Team talk
The team gathers in the locker room for a final pep talk. The referee asks the teams to line up in the tunnel five minutes before kick off.

6 Sporting gesture
The two teams run onto the field and shake hands. The players then take their position on the field.

7 Kick off
A coin toss decides which team kicks off from the center circle. The referee blows the whistle and the game gets underway.

Caught **offside**

An **attacker** is in an **offside position** if he or she steps closer to the **opponent's goal** than any of the **defenders** before the ball is **kicked to the player**. The rule stops attackers from **hanging** near to the goal.

Although this player is in an offside position, it is not an offside infringement because the player is not active in play.

ACTIVE IN PLAY

A player can only be offside if he or she receives the ball in the opposition's half of the field. The player must also be active in the play, or be giving the team an advantage by being in that position.

In this game scenario, the attacking player passes the ball to a teammate who is in an offside positon. The team is immediately penalized and the opposition wins an indrect free kick.

An attacker is **not offside** if he or she **receives the ball from a corner, throw-in, or goal kick.**

Player A stays onside, as he is level with the defender closest to the goal line.

2. Player B is offside. He is closer to the opposition goal than any of the defenders when he receives the pass and becomes active in play.

3. The assistant referee stands in line with the defender closest to the goal. The official raises the flag to signal that an attacking player is offside.

Ⓑ

Ⓐ

1. The attacker puts the team in an offside position by passing the ball to player B. The pass should have been made to player A instead.

The line of offside is based on the position of the defender who is closest to the team's goal line.

4. The referee spots the assistant referee's offside signal and stops play. The defending team will be awarded an indirect free kick.

📊 **FAST FACTS**

Originally, the offside rule forced attackers to stay in front of two defenders. The rule was revised to a single defender in 1925, and led to a 36 percent increase in the number of goals across the English leagues in the following season.

1924–25 season

1925–26 season

4,700 goals

6,373 goals

What is a foul?

The rules state that soccer must be played **fairly** and **safely**. It is the **referee's** job to call a **foul** if a player commits an **unfair act**, and to award the opposition a **free kick**— or a **penalty** if the foul occured in the penalty box.

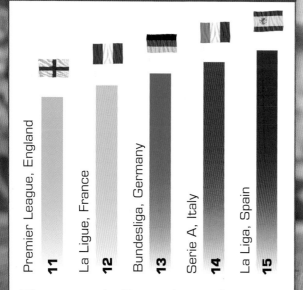

FAST FACTS

Premier League, England **11**

La Ligue, France **12**

Bundesliga, Germany **13**

Serie A, Italy **14**

La Liga, Spain **15**

The teams in Europe's top five leagues commit between 11 and 15 fouls per game. The English Premier League records the lowest number. This is perhaps because the referees are more lenient.

COMMON FOULS

A foul can be committed in a number of ways. Below are among the most common:

Handball
Deliberately using
the hand to
control the ball.

Obstruction
Blocking an
opponent without
making any attempt
to play the ball.

Tripping
Intentionally
tripping up
an opponent.

Holding
Pulling on an
opponent's shirt
to slow him down.

Dangerous play
Making a
reckless tackle
that endangers
a player's safety.

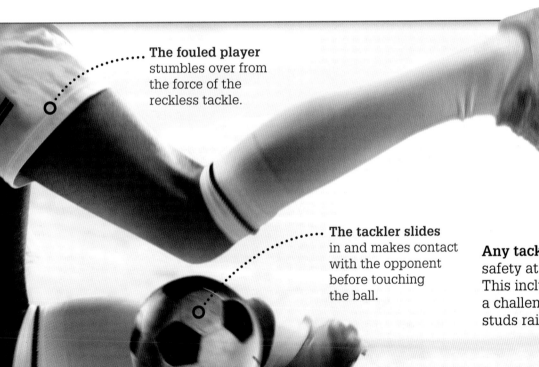

The fouled player
stumbles over from
the force of the
reckless tackle.

The tackler slides
in and makes contact
with the opponent
before touching
the ball.

Any tackle that puts player
safety at risk is a serious foul.
This includes sliding in to make
a challenge with the cleat
studs raised.

Brazil made
**31 fouls in a
game versus
Columbia in the
FIFA 2014
World Cup.**

Free kicks

A team wins a **free kick** whenever the opposition commits a **foul** outside their own penalty area. The free kick is taken from the **spot** where the offense occurred and, if it is close to the opponent's goal, can present a good **goal-scoring** chance.

If a team shoots a free kick into its own goal, the opposition is awarded a corner.

Curving shot

The goalkeeper guards the area around the post closest to him.

TYPES OF FREE KICK

Signal for a direct free kick.

Signal for an indirect free kick.

There are two types of free kick—direct and indirect. The referee awards a direct free kick against a foul, whereas an indirect free kick results from a technical infringement. Direct free kicks can be shot straight into goal, but an indirect free kick must be touched by a teammate first.

In this direct free kick, the player has a shot on goal. It is up to him to decide where to direct the shot, and then either drill, curve, spin, or apply dip to the ball.

SHOOTING OPTIONS

Curving shot
The free kick taker strikes across the ball with the side of the foot. This applies spin and makes the ball curve in the air.

Dipping shot
In this type of free kick, the player puts top spin on the ball by striking it with the laces and then shortening the follow-through.

Through the wall
The player shoots the ball low and fast underneath the wall. This may catch the defenders off-guard, who leap up expecting an aerial shot.

The defensive wall is made up of several players who stand in a line to guard the goal. They must be at least 10 yd (9 m) away from the ball.

Dipping shot

Curving shot

Through the wall

The free kick taker is a specialist who can direct the shot with pace and accuracy.

The top left-hand corner of the goal is the natural side for the right-footed player to aim.

The inner arc (red) represents the goalkeeper's "diving envelope." Any shots placed in this area are within his reach and will be saved if he dives the right way.

The average speed of a penalty is 70 mph (112 km/h).

SENSATIONAL SHOOTOUT

The 1994 FIFA World Cup final was the first to be decided by a penalty shootout. Brazil won the game after Italy's star player, Roberto Baggio, ballooned the decisive penalty over the bar.

Goalkeepers will choose the right way to dive 70 percent of the time, according to statistics.

The orange arc represents a zone in which the goalkeeper can still reach the ball by diving. Any shots placed here can still be saved.

Penalties placed in the top corners are unsaveable, even by world-class goalkeepers. However, they carry a higher risk of missing the target.

That gives a goalkeeper **only 700 milliseconds** to save it.

A penalty shootout in the **2005 Namibian Cup** finished **17–16**.

Deciding where to place the ball when taking a penalty depends on a number of factors. Are you right- or left-footed? Is the goalkeeper right- or left-handed? How much of a risk are you prepared to take?

Taking penalties

The penalty kick is one of the most dramatic moments in a soccer game. A **single kick** from the **penalty spot** can determine which team **wins or loses** the game, or even the entire league.

Corners

A team wins a **corner** whenever the ball **crosses the byline** after touching an opposition player. A corner presents a chance to play the ball into a **good attacking** position.

From a corner, the ball can be played anywhere on the field, but the corner taker typically chooses either the far post, the near post, the penalty spot, or to the closest teammate. The aim is to create the best opportunity to score.

The corner taker is the team's dead-ball specialist, who is skilled at delivering the ball with great accuracy.

Far post corner

Near post corner

Penalty spot corner

The ball must be placed on or behind the corner arc marking.

📈 FAST FACTS

From the 13,000 corners taken taken in the English Premier League over two seasons (2011–13), 2,150 led to a shot attempt, of which only 370 resulted in a goal—equating to about three percent.

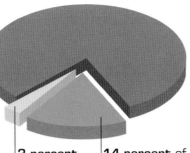

83 percent of corners cleared

3 percent goals scored

14 percent of shots saved

TYPES OF CORNER

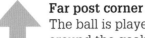

Far post corner
The ball is played into the area around the goalpost that is furthest away from the corner taker.

Near post corner
The ball is kicked to a tall teammate positioned at the goal closest to the corner arc, who uses the head to flick the ball across goal into a striker's path.

Penalty spot corner
The ball is delivered to an unmarked attacker in the penalty area who is in a position to shoot.

Short corner
The ball is passed to the nearest teammate who is in a better position to cross the ball into the penalty area.

Players aiming to score from a corner move around in the penalty area to get away from their marker.

One goal was scored from every 70 corners taken at the 2010 FIFA World Cup.

Short corner

The card system

If a player commits a **serious foul**, the referee shows the **offender** a card. A **yellow card** serves as a warning, whereas a **red card** means the player must leave the pitch right away.

English referee **Ken Aston** invented the **card system** after the 1966 FIFA World Cup.

The referee points to the dressing room immediately after showing the offender a red card. According to the laws, the sent-off player cannot remain on—or anywhere around—the field of play.

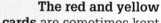

The red and yellow cards are sometimes kept in different pockets, so the referee avoids pulling out the wrong card in the heat of the moment.

REFEREE'S NOTEBOOK

The referee uses a notebook to record key facts and incidents that occur in the game. This includes goal times, details of any substitutions made, and the names of players who have received a red or yellow card.

The sent-off player cannot be replaced. The team must play the rest of the game with one fewer player.

📈 FAST FACTS

A player receives a yellow card for offenses, such as those listed opposite. A red card is shown for very serious offenses, such as those listed below.

Yellow card offenses

- Rough tackling
- Arguing with the referee
- Holding an opponent
- Blocking the goalkeeper
- Deliberate timewasting
- Refusing to move the correct distance from a free kick
- Deliberate handball
- Unsporting behavior

Red card offenses

- Dangerous tackling
- Violent conduct
- Using bad language
- Spitting at an opponent or any other person
- Denying the opposition a goal-scoring chance with a deliberate foul
- Receiving a second yellow card

Goal line technology

Goal line technology (GLT) is a **computerized system** introduced in 2012 to help officials in situations when it is difficult to tell whether or not the **ball has crossed the goal line** for a goal.

HOW IT WORKS:

1 Seven fast frame cameras located above and around each goal track the ball's movement in the goal area.

2 The cameras send the information to a computer that analyzes if the ball has crossed the goal line.

Goal line technology is able to relay the result to the referee within a second of the incident taking place, which means there is no delay to the game.

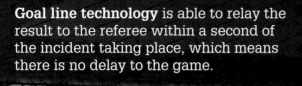

COSTLY ERRORS

Following several refereeing errors at the 2010 FIFA World Cup—including a disallowed England goal in their 4–1 defeat to Germany (above)—FIFA decided to bring in goal line technology.

The GLT system only **relays** information to the game officials.

📊 FAST FACTS

A goal is awarded when the officials are sure that every part of the ball has crossed the goal line. Goal line technology is highly accurate, with a margin of error of only 0.12 in (3 mm).

Goal line

Field

Goal

Goal line

Field

No Goal

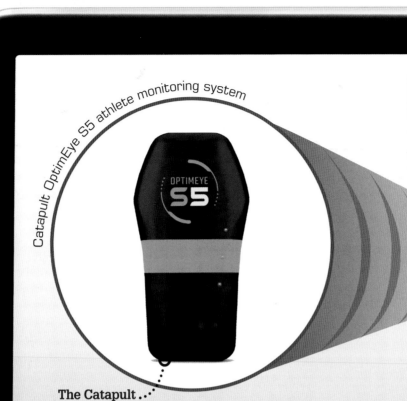

Catapult OptimEye S5 athlete monitoring system

The Catapult device can analyze 1,000 items of data every second.

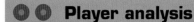

The tracking device is placed between a player's shoulders. It gathers huge amounts of information, which can be analyzed both during and after the game.

Tracking players

Many players wear a **tracking device** under their shirt. This provides **crucial information** about the player's **physical performance**.

PRECISION PASSING

Every pass a player makes in a game is also recorded. Blue arrows are successful passes; red arrows are unsuccessful ones.

Data recieved

Heart rate
A program analyzes a player's heart rate during a game. Using this data, analysts can tell when players start to tire.

Number of sprints
The number of sprints a player makes in a game is tracked. A drop in number may indicate player fatigue or injury.

Yards per minute
Logging the amount of ground a player covers every minute reveals a player's overall fitness or stamina.

Total distance covered
The device also tracks the total amount of ground a player covers during the course of a game.

High-speed running
Analysts can tell the total distance a player has sprinted in a game. The higher the number, the fitter the player.

Acceleration
The device measures the total number of accelerations a player makes in a game, how long they last, and how much ground is covered.

Dynamic stress load
By tracking a player's movement the device calculates how hard the player is working throughout the match.

Deceleration
The total number of times a player slows down in a game is logged, and how much ground is covered.

Over time

Gerardo Bedoya

has received **more red cards** than any other player in professional soccer. Capped **49 times** for Colombia, the defensive midfielder picked up **46 red cards** in a **20-year career** between 1995 and 2015.

BEDOYA
46

Red cards only became **compulsory** in **every** soccer game in **1982.**

Total **red cards** at the FIFA World Cup:

Brazil—11
☐☐☐☐☐☐☐☐☐☐☐

Argentina—10
☐☐☐☐☐☐☐☐☐☐

Uruguay—9
☐☐☐☐☐☐☐☐☐

Cameroon—8
☐☐☐☐☐☐☐☐

Italy—8
☐☐☐☐☐☐☐☐

The record for the *fastest dismissal* in a professional game is held by Bologna's **Giuseppe Lorenzo**. He was sent off after 10 seconds in an Italian Serie A game against Parma in 1990 for hitting an opponent.

00:10

Team shirt sales

Manchester United sells more replica shirts per year than any other club in world soccer.

1
Manchester United
1,750,000

2
Real Madrid
1,650,000

3
Barcelona
1,278,000

4
Bayern Munich
1,200,000

5
Chelsea
899,000

Colombia's Marcos Coll **is the only player** to score **directly from a corner** in a *FIFA World Cup final game*. He scored the wonder goal against the *Soviet Union*, at the **1962** tournament in Chile.

The longest

penalty shootout of all time in professional soccer occurred in a game between KK Palace and Civics in the Namibian Cup final in 2005. Forty-eight spot kicks were taken before KK Palace finally triumphed 17–16.

Shirt sponsorship

Shirt sponsorship has become a major source of revenue for clubs around the world, but the amount of money raised in this way varies from league to league. England's Premier League leads the way.

On wet, *rainy days,* leather soccer balls **could often double** in weight. **By the** *end of a game* **the ball could weigh as much as** **2.2 lb (1 kg).**

$292 million

$130 million

$106 million

$90 million

$79 million

| Premier League **England** | Bundesliga **Germany** | La Liga **Spain** | Ligue 1 **France** | Serie A **Italy** |

Individual skills

Soccer is a fast-paced game in which players must have the skills to control the ball's movement. These skills include passing, shooting, tackling, volleying, heading, and dribbling. To be able to use these skills automatically in games, players practice them regularly in training.

Ball control

Any player who receives the ball must be able to bring it **under control** right away. The **quicker** the player can do this, the more **time and space** there will be to decide the next move.

1. Chest trap
Lean back and cushion the ball with the chest. The key is to slow the ball's speed at the point of contact.

2. Balance
Use the arms for balance and also to shield the ball from any opponents.

3. Ball position
As the ball drops to the ground in front of you, get ready to make a pass or run with the ball.

The quality of the "first touch" determines how quickly a player can control the ball. The best players can put the ball exactly where they want it with a single touch.

Professional players use an average of two touches per possession.

SKILL DRILL

In tight situations, use the top of the foot to control a ball that arrives at shin height, so you can make a pass or start a dribble.

Closely watch the ball as it comes to your foot.

Relax the foot as the ball lands on it.

Passing

Passing is the most **efficient way** of **moving the ball** toward the opponent's goal. Skilled players are able to make passes accurately along the **ground**, in the **air**, and over a **range** of distances.

The short pass is the most accurate form of passing, in which the passer plays the ball to a teammate who is nearby.

The passing player strikes the ball with the side of his foot to make a short pass, the laces of the cleat for a long pass, and the outside of the foot for a wide, diagonal pass.

SKILL DRILL

A short pass is a controlled pass made with the side of the foot. In this form of passing, the ball is kicked to a teammate along the ground and moves at a relatively slow speed.

1. Point the standing foot in the direction you want the ball to travel and strike the ball with the side of the foot.

Keep ankle locked at the point of contact.

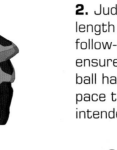

2. Judge the length of the follow-through to ensure that the ball has enough pace to reach the intended target.

Sweep the striking foot across.

The player making the pass must be able to control the ball's speed and direction so that it reaches the intended teammate without being blocked by an opponent.

The long ball is played over a large distance toward the opponent's goal, in the hope that a teammate receives the ball and starts an attack.

The wide, diagonal pass is a long-range pass, normally made from inside the player's own half to a teammate near the touchline.

A long ball describes any pass that is longer than 35 yd (32 m).

TIKI-TAKA

Tiki-taka is a style of play in which a team passes and moves at high speed, denying the opposition possession of the ball. The style was introduced in the mid-2000s by Spanish club Barcelona, who won the Champions League trophy three times between 2008 and 2015.

Dribbling

The ability to move the ball past opposing players in tight spaces is known as **dribbling**. Good dribblers have **quick feet**, **great balance**, and create more goal-scoring chances.

The best dribblers keep the ball close to their feet. They move the ball using the inside and outside of both feet, as they twist and turn their way past defenders.

A player **dribbles** the ball an average distance of **208 yards (191 m)** in a game.

DRIBBLING DYNAMO

During the 1986 FIFA World Cup quarter-final game against England, Argentina's star player Diego Maradona dribbled past five English players to score one of the most impressive goals in World Cup history.

1. Look ahead
Assess the situation in front as you move forward with the ball.

2. Shoulder feint
Drop the shoulder as though you are about to move in one direction, but take the ball the opposite way.

SKILL DRILL

The step over is a trick used to fool an opponent into thinking you're about to make a pass when the real aim is to dribble past them.

Drop shoulder

1. Approach the ball as if you are about to pass it with the outside of the foot.

Place weight on the non-kicking foot

Look straight ahead

Swivel the foot around the ball

2. Instead of passing, move the foot around the ball and then dribble in the opposite direction.

3. Beat the opponent
Use the outside of your foot to move the ball away from the challenger. Keep the ball close to your feet.

Shooting

If you want to be the team's **star goal scorer**, you will need **accurate shooting** skills. There are many shot types, but the most spectacular is the **power shot**, where a player **strikes the ball hard**, and hopes the **ball's speed** and direction will take it past the goalkeeper.

When taking a power shot, aim to kick the ball either side of the goalkeeper. The hardest places for the keeper to reach are the four corners of the net.

1. Ball-watching
Keep your eyes focused on the part of the ball you want to strike.

2. Body position
Keep your upper body over the ball during the shot so the ball stays low.

Fewer than **three out of every 20 goal-scoring attempts result in a goal.**

5. Impact
Make firm contact with the bottom right part of the ball and follow through with the kicking leg.

3. Standing leg
Line up the non-kicking foot alongside the ball with the toe pointing in the direction you want to aim the shot.

4. Striking leg
Sweep the shooting leg smoothly and strike the ball with the instep for an inswinging shot.

GOAL MACHINE

Brazilian legend Pele was among the finest goalscorers ever. In a glittering career that spanned 22 years (1955–77), he played 1,363 games and scored an amazing 1,281 goals.

Volleying

Striking the ball while it is in midair is known as volleying. Watching a player volley the ball into the **back of the net** is one of the most **stunning sights** in soccer.

3. Impact
Strike the ball firmly with the top of the cleat.

4. Leg position
Keep the striking leg parallel to the ground during the follow through.

LONGEST VOLLEY

During a German league game in 2014, SC Paderborn's player Moritz Stoppelkamp volleyed the ball 90 yards (82 meters) into an empty net to score the longest volleyed goal ever.

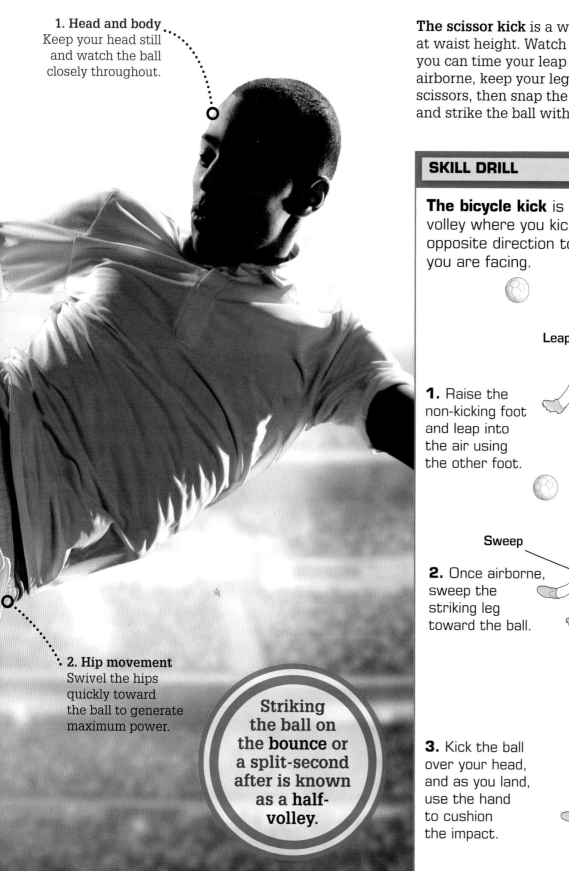

1. Head and body
Keep your head still and watch the ball closely throughout.

2. Hip movement
Swivel the hips quickly toward the ball to generate maximum power.

Striking the ball on the **bounce** or a split-second after is known as a **half-volley**.

The scissor kick is a way of volleying a ball at waist height. Watch the ball's flight so you can time your leap correctly. While airborne, keep your legs apart like open scissors, then snap the kicking leg forward and strike the ball with power.

SKILL DRILL

The bicycle kick is an overhead volley where you kick the ball in the opposite direction to that in which you are facing.

Leap

1. Raise the non-kicking foot and leap into the air using the other foot.

Sweep

2. Once airborne, sweep the striking leg toward the ball.

Strike

3. Kick the ball over your head, and as you land, use the hand to cushion the impact.

Heading

Heading the ball is a vital skill for both **attackers** and **defenders**. Players who are expert headers **score more goals**, defend better, and win more battles for **possession**.

Giant leap
Time your leap correctly so that you meet the ball before any opposition players.

A HEAD FOR GOAL

In the 2002 FIFA World Cup tournament, German forward Miroslav Klose scored five goals in total—all of them were headers.

Firm contact
Use the forehead. This provides the most accuracy and power.

Pull up
Use your arms to pull yourself as high into the air as possible.

SKILL DRILL

When making a defensive header, the main aim is to knock the ball as far away as possible from the attacking player.

Use your forehead.

Leap up to meet the ball.

For a power header, the player leaps in the air and uses the neck muscles to sling his forehead to make contact with the ball.

Some players are able to leap up to **8 ft (2.4 m)** to head the ball.

⬔ FAST FACTS

The chart opposite shows the number of different types of challenge a defender typically makes to dispossess the opponent in a game.

Tackle	⚽ ⚽ ⚽ 3
Header challenge	⚽ 1
Pressing opponent	⚽ 1
Blocking a shot or pass	⚽ ⚽ ⚽ ⚽ ⚽ ⚽ ⚽ ⚽ ⚽ ⚽ ⚽ ⚽ ⚽ ⚽ ⚽ ⚽ ⚽ ⚽ ⚽ 19
Clearing a long ball	⚽ 1

The slide tackle is used by defenders as a last-ditch effort to dispossess an opponent, as the tackler ends up on the ground and out of the game. Unless the tackle is accurate, there is also a high chance of fouling (and even injuring) the attacker.

1. Leg position
Slide in with the tackling leg and knock the ball away from the attacker.

SKILL DRILL

The block tackle is the safest type of tackle. To make this tackle, meet the attacker head on and block the ball as soon as the attacker tries to shoot or make a pass.

1. Stand in front of your opponent to deny him room.

2. Block the kick and make sure you keep the ankle firm.

Tackling

A tackle is made to dispossess an **opponent**. The player must know how and when to make the tackle, so the ball is **won cleanly** without **fouling** or **injuring** the opponent.

The world's top defenders make about **5 tackles** in a game.

3. Perfect timing
Watch the ball closely to make sure you take it cleanly from the opponent.

2. Support
Use the arms to support the body on the ground.

Over-time

Belgian goalkeeper **Kristof von Hout** is officially the world's tallest-ever player, measuring **6.8 ft** (2.08 m). Brazilian midfielder **Elton Gomes** is the **shortest,** standing at **5.05 ft** (154 cm).

Across the five top European leagues, *the* **passing accuracy** averages out to **76.1 percent.** Below are the individual percentages for each of the five leagues.

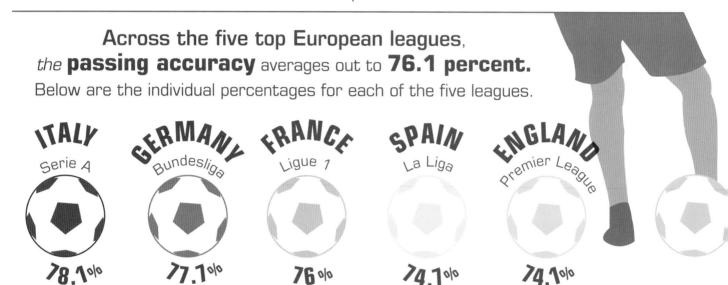

ITALY
Serie A
78.1%

GERMANY
Bundesliga
77.1%

FRANCE
Ligue 1
76%

SPAIN
La Liga
74.1%

ENGLAND
Premier League
74.1%

The longest kick to **score a goal** was achieved by Bosnian goalkeeper **Asmir Begovic** during an **English Premier League game. Begovic's** strike was officially measured at **100 yd** (91.9 m).

At elite level, **62** percent of *all goals scored* are from **open play. Free kicks** and **corners** account for **30** percent, and penalties make up **8** percent.

Open play
62

8
Penalties

30

Free kicks and corners

A goal in every minute!

Star strikers Cristiano Ronaldo and **Zlatan Ibrahimovic** have **both** scored in **each minute**, from the **1st** to the **90th**, in competitive soccer.

The world record for the **longest headed goal** is 63.4 yd (58 m) scored by Odd's BK's **Joan Samuelsen** in 2011 against Tromso in the **Norwegian Eliteserien** league.

The **best way** to spend the 15-minute halftime interval is to *rest* for the first **7.5 minutes** and then use the **other half** to do *light activity* to warm up the **muscles**.

Borussia Dortmund's **Pierre-Emerick Aubameyang** is the world's fastest player. He is said to have run **40 yd (30 m)** in a staggering **3.7 seconds** during training!

The most goals scored by a **single player** in a FIFA *World Cup finals* *tournament* was **13** by **Just Fontaine** of France in 1958.

A team game

Soccer is a team game of 11 players, who must work together to beat the opposition. The manager helps them to achieve this by making sure they practice hard on the training field, by picking a formation to suit the players' strengths, and by making sure that the 11 players know their roles.

Goalkeeping

The goalkeeper is allowed to **handle** the ball inside the team's **penalty area**, but nowhere else on the field. As the team's last line of defense, this key player has to be **quick** and good at **leaping**, **catching**, and **kicking**.

HIGH ACHIEVER

Spanish goalkeeper Iker Casillas won many trophies with his club team Real Madrid between the years 1999 and 2015. This includes five league titles, four Spanish Cups, two Champions League trophies, the Copa Del Rey, and the UEFA Super Cup.

Pay close attention to the game, anticipate any dangers, and be ready to stop any shots.

Stay on your toes at all times, so you can leap in either direction to make a save.

The goalkeeper must always be ready to make a diving save, as skillful attackers tend to direct their shots into the corners of the goal.

Reach the ball with an outstretched hand and push it out of play.

Keep the wrist locked to keep the ball from slipping through the hands.

USA keeper Tim Howard made 15 saves vs Belgium at the 2014 FIFA World Cup.

MARSHALLING THE DEFENSE

The goalkeeper is not just a shot-stopper, but also the leader in defense. It is the goalkeeper's job to organize the defenders so they can deal with any threats to goal. When defending free kicks, the goalkeeper forms the defensive wall by telling the defenders where to stand.

Fullback

Fullbacks operate on either side of the field and defend the touchline. When one fullback goes on a forward run, the other will move across to support the center backs.

Wingback

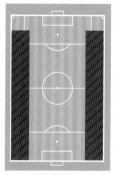

Two wingbacks operate on either side of the field, but slightly up the field compared to the fullback. Wingbacks are responsible for both attacking and defending along the touchline.

GAME STATS
Distance: 6.2 miles (10.0 km)
Tackles: 2.0
Passes: 41.2
Clearances: 3.2

ATTACK

DEFENSE

DEFENSE

DEFENSE

DEFENSE

ATTACK

GAME STATS
Distance: 5.9 miles (9.5 km)
Tackles: 1.7
Passes: 41.9
Clearances: 5.9

DEFENSE

The sweeper used to be an important position in the past, but is rarely seen in the modern game. Not a single team used one at the 2014 FIFA World Cup.

DEFENSE

DEFENSE

DEFENSE

Center back

A team places two center backs in front of the goalkeeper. They mark the opposition's most advanced forwards, and their main role is to clear the ball from the penalty area.

Sweeper

The sweeper is usually placed behind the center backs. He has no marking duties, so may move forward when his team is in possession. The use of a sweeper has fallen out of fashion in recent times.

Dutch center back Ronald Koeman scored **253 goals** in his career—**a record for a defender**.

ATTACK

THE GREAT DEFENDER

A FIFA World Cup winner with West Germany in 1974, Franz Beckenbauer is considered one of the greatest defenders in soccer history. He redefined the role of a sweeper, from simply being a defensive stopper to becoming a team's creative attacking force.

ATTACK

ATTACK

GAME STATS
Distance: 6.6 miles (10.6 km)
Tackles: 1.5
Passes: 34.8
Dribbles: 2.1

ATTACK

Solid defending

A defender's main job is **to stop the opponent from scoring a goal**. There are **four types** of defender: fullback, wingback, center back, and sweeper (also known as a "libero").

Defenders must operate as a unit, but each has a different role to play. Fullbacks make the most tackles, center backs execute the most clearances, while wingbacks have to run the furthest.

Defensive midfielder

This player's role is to stop an opponent's attack, and to cover in defense if one of his team's defenders joins an attack. Defensive midfielders will rarely advance into an opponent's half.

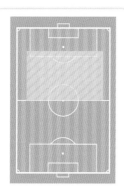

Central midfielder

In attack, central midfielders pass the ball and look to join the forwards. In defense, they drop back to help the defenders stop an opponent's attack.

GAME STATS
Distance: 5.5 miles (8.9 km)
Tackles: 5.5
Passes: 48.6
Dribbles: 0.9

GAME STATS
Distance: 6.4 miles (10.3 km)
Tackles: 2.4
Passes: 47.3
Dribbles: 1.2

GAME STATS
Distance: 5.7 miles (9.1 km)
Tackles: 2.1
Passes: 43.0
Dribbles: 1.6

Barcelona's Xavi made a world record **125 passes** against Espanyol in 2014–15.

Midfield magic

Midfielders **break up** an opponent's play and **set in motion** their own team's attack. There are **four types of midfielder**: defensive midfielder, central midfielder, wide midfielder, and attacking midfielder.

Wide midfielder
A wide midfielder is positioned closer to the touchline. In attack, their main role is to provide crosses into the opponent's penalty area. In defense, they must drop back to provide extra cover.

Attacking midfielder
The attacking midfielder is the creative force of a team and a link between the midfield and a striker. Attacking midfielders only have a limited defensive role and rarely drop back in their own half.

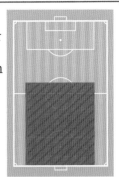

Midfielders have a crucial role to play in both defense and attack, with each type of player having to perform different tasks. Defensive midfielders average the most tackles per game, while central midfielders run the furthest. The number of midfield players a team fields depends on its formation.

DEFENSE

ATTACK

ATTACK

ATTACK

ATTACK

ATTACK

GAME STATS
Distance: 6.3 miles (10.1 km)
Tackles: 1.7
Passes: 39.5
Dribbles: 1.3

MIDFIELD MASTER

Johan Cruyff was the best midfielder of his generation. During his 20-year career, he won eight Dutch league titles, one Spanish league title, and led the Netherlands to the FIFA World Cup final in 1974.

Flying forwards

Forwards are the players who are positioned **closest to an opponent's goal**. Their main job is to **score goals**, and they are often a team's most-celebrated, and expensive, players.

DEFENSE

ATTACK

DEFENSE

Forwards have to be **fast**. Some can run as fast as **10.6 yd (9.7 m) per second.**

GAME STATS
Distance: 5.8 miles (9.4 km)
Tackles: 0.9
Passes: 28.5
Shots: 1.5

No.10/Second striker
The No.10 (also known as the second striker), plays in the space between an opponent's defense and midfield, commonly known as "the hole." From there, they will set up attacks or shoot for goal.

Winger
Part of an attacking formation, a winger is responsible for attacking down the edges of the field and for sending crosses into the penalty box. Wingers have limited defensive duties.

Center forward

A center forward's main job is to score goals and so they spend most of their time operating in an area in front of the opponent's goal. From here, they are in the best position to receive balls, turn, and score.

TOP STRIKE PARTNERSHIP

Two of the greatest forwards the game has ever seen, Alfredo Di Stéfano (left) and Ferenc Puskás combined with devastating effect for Real Madrid. Together, they propelled the Spanish giants to four consecutive league titles (1961–64) and two European Cups (1959 and 1960), and scored a staggering 258 goals in 182 league games.

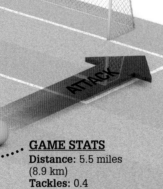

ATTACK

ATTACK

ATTACK

DEFENSE

GAME STATS
Distance: 5.5 miles (8.9 km)
Tackles: 0.4
Passes: 18.3
Shots: 2.1

GAME STATS
Distance: 5.8 miles (9.3 km)
Tackles: 1.0
Passes: 25.7
Shots: 1.7

Forwards have many different roles. Center forwards average the most shots per game. No.10s and wingers have to create goal-scoring opportunities for the center forward.

Formations

A formation is the **way a team lines up on the field**. It is normally **described using a string of numbers**, which represent the number of players in each area of the field.

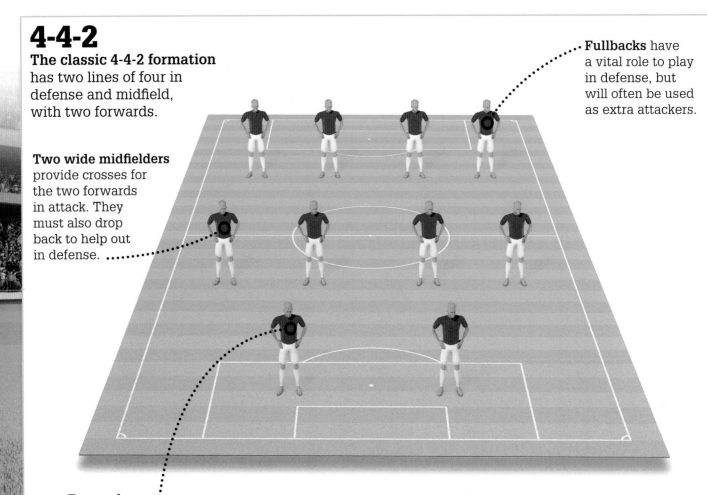

AC Milan won **the Champions League in 1989 and 1990** using a **4-4-2**.

4-4-2

The classic 4-4-2 formation has two lines of four in defense and midfield, with two forwards.

Two wide midfielders provide crosses for the two forwards in attack. They must also drop back to help out in defense.

Fullbacks have a vital role to play in defense, but will often be used as extra attackers.

Forwards can advance to the opponent's goal without having to wait for support from the midfield.

✔ Advantages

- Two lines of four provide greater defensive cover.
- A pair of strikers creates a constant attacking threat.
- Fullbacks provide extra width to stretch an opponent's defense.

✘ Disadvantages

- With only two central midfielders, a team can easily be outnumbered in midfield.
- Opponent can exploit the space between defense and midfield—called "the hole."
- This system places great pressure on midfielders both to attack and defend.

4-2-3-1

The dominant formation at the turn of the 21st century, this is still the preferred system in much of Europe.

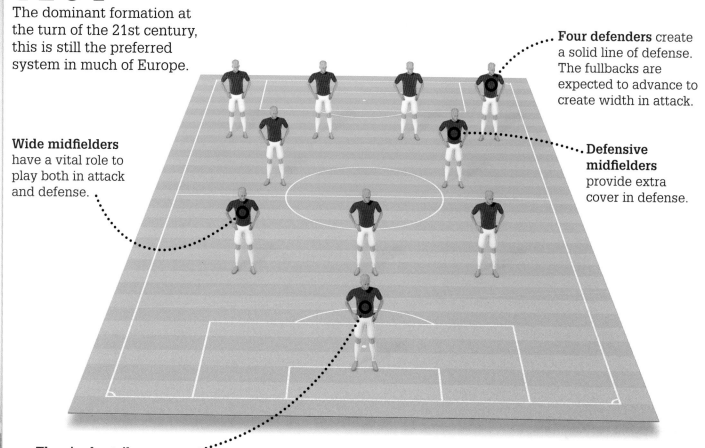

Four defenders create a solid line of defense. The fullbacks are expected to advance to create width in attack.

Defensive midfielders provide extra cover in defense.

Wide midfielders have a vital role to play both in attack and defense.

The single striker relies on support from the three attacking midfielders.

✔ Advantages

- It is easy to pass the ball through midfield.
- This system makes it hard for teams to be overrun in midfield.
- Three attacking midfielders provide a greater number of attacking options.

✗ Disadvantages

- The single striker relies on support from attacking midfielders.
- Attacking midfielders have to work very hard to cover in both defense and attack.
- This system places great responsibility on the wide players to drop back to help out in defense.

Other modern formations

4-1-2-1-2
Also known as "The Diamond," this formation provides greater solidity in midfield. Fullbacks can move forward to provide the width in attack.

4-3-2-1
Named the "Christmas Tree" after its pointed shape, this is a more attacking variation of the 4-3-3, with two players playing behind a single striker.

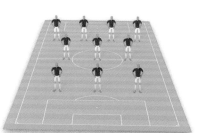

4-3-3
Three midfielders move across the field as a unit. Because it has more attackers, many teams adopt this system if they are chasing a game.

More formations

4-5-1

A packed midfield means this is the formation of choice for teams looking to avoid defeat in knockout competitions.

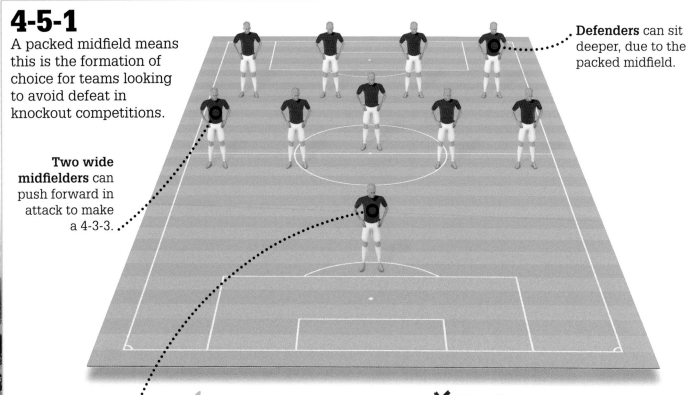

Defenders can sit deeper, due to the packed midfield.

Two wide midfielders can push forward in attack to make a 4-3-3.

A single striker has to keep possession of the ball in attack and wait for support.

✔ Advantages

- A five-player midfield normally leads to more possession of the ball.
- The formation is flexible. For example, it is easy to switch to a 4-3-3 in attack.
- This is a difficult formation for an opponent to break down.

✗ Disadvantages

- It is easy for the single striker to become isolated.
- The formation makes it difficult for teams to execute counterattacks.
- Great pressure is placed on central midfielders to join the striker in attack.

BRAZIL BREAKS THE MOLD

Developed to strengthen the defense without losing any numbers in attack, the 4-2-4 formation burst onto the scene when Brazil won the 1958 FIFA World Cup. In practice, it operates as a 4-3-3 in defense and as a 3-3-4 in attack.

Many think a 4-6-0 formation, with no striker, will be the **formation of the future.**

5-3-2/3-5-2

A pair of wingbacks provides extra options in both defense and attack, but they have to be incredibly fit to make the formation work.

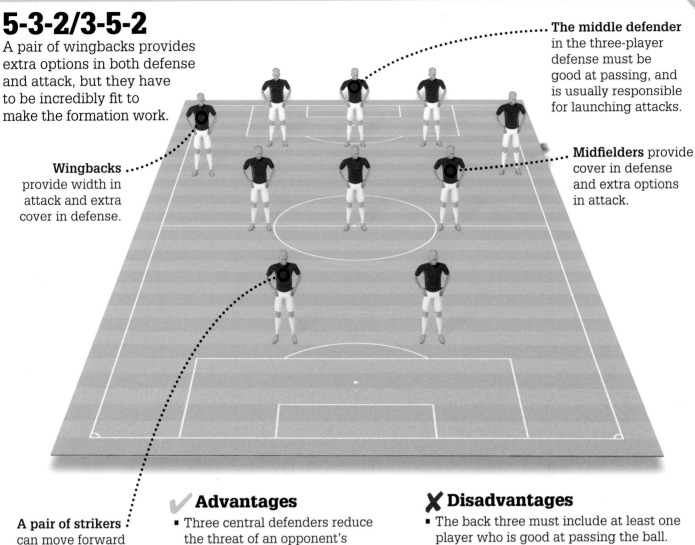

The middle defender in the three-player defense must be good at passing, and is usually responsible for launching attacks.

Wingbacks provide width in attack and extra cover in defense.

Midfielders provide cover in defense and extra options in attack.

A pair of strikers can move forward to attack without having to wait for extra support from midfield.

✔ Advantages

- Three central defenders reduce the threat of an opponent's counterattack.
- The defensive unit is usually helped by a deep-lying midfielder.
- Three midfielders and wingbacks provide a variety of attacking options.

✗ Disadvantages

- The back three must include at least one player who is good at passing the ball.
- Players require a superb sense of positioning to play in this formation.

Old formations

2-3-5
Known as "The Pyramid," this was the standard formation of the 1880s. It placed a huge emphasis on attacking.

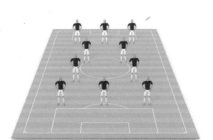

3-2-2-3 (also known as WM)
First used in the 1920s, this formation reinforced the defense to counter the increased attacking threat that came about from a change in the offside rule.

Sweeper

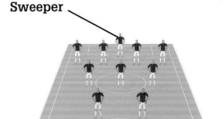

1-4-3-2
Known as "catenaccio," this formation saw a sweeper (or "libero") positioned between the goalkeeper and the defense to add more defensive steel.

Set pieces: attacking

Corners and **free kicks** are called **set pieces**. They provide teams with the perfect opportunity to **execute set moves** they have spent **hours rehearsing** on the training ground.

The attacking side will often position a player in front of the near post. This player will look to flick the ball on with his head.

Where the corner taker delivers the ball will depend on the set move planned.

📈 **FAST FACTS**

Although corners represent a good goal-scoring opportunity, not as many goals are scored from them as you might think.

5
Average number of corners a team wins in a game.

75
One in 75 corners taken leads directly to a goal.

45
One in 45 corners taken leads indirectly to a goal.

6%
Percentage of goals scored from corners at the 2010 FIFA World Cup.

The players who are the best headers in the attacking team will line up near the edge of the penalty area and run toward goal as the corner is taken.

At least one player is left near the edge of the penalty area to pounce on any rebounds. They could also be a set move option for the corner taker.

Set piece: free kick

If a free kick is awarded too far away for a direct shot on goal, the attacking side will look to use a set move they have practiced on the training ground.

Option 1: Clipped cross
The free kick taker will look to swing the ball toward the edge of the six-yard box. Attackers will run toward the goal to meet the incoming ball.

Option 2: Short pass
The free kick taker plays a short pass to a teammate, who runs to the byline before crossing the ball.

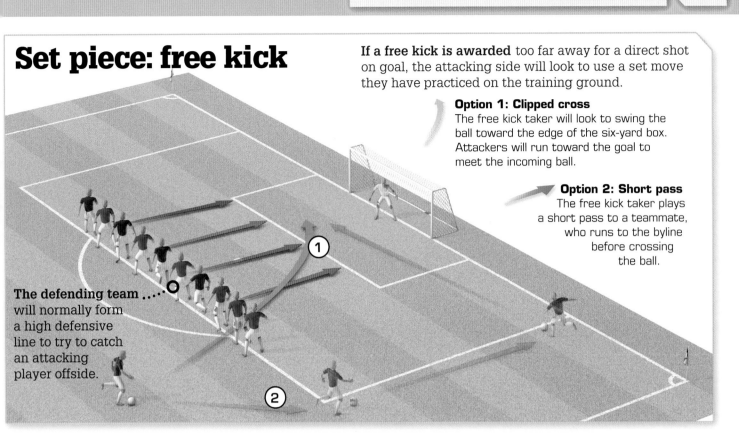

The defending team will normally form a high defensive line to try to catch an attacking player offside.

One attacking player will look to block the goalkeeper.

The defenders in this scenario are using the zonal defense system.

Set piece: corner
The attacking team will set up in the same way for most corners. Where the ball is delivered will depend on the set move the attacking side has chosen to execute.

One in five goals scored in professional soccer comes from a set piece.

Another attacking player will make a run toward the far post, in case the corner taker delivers a long corner.

Set pieces: defending

Because **set pieces** offer such a good goal-scoring opportunity, it is **vital that a defense is organized** to deal with the impending threat.

Teams use two main systems when they are defending corners: zonal marking or man marking.

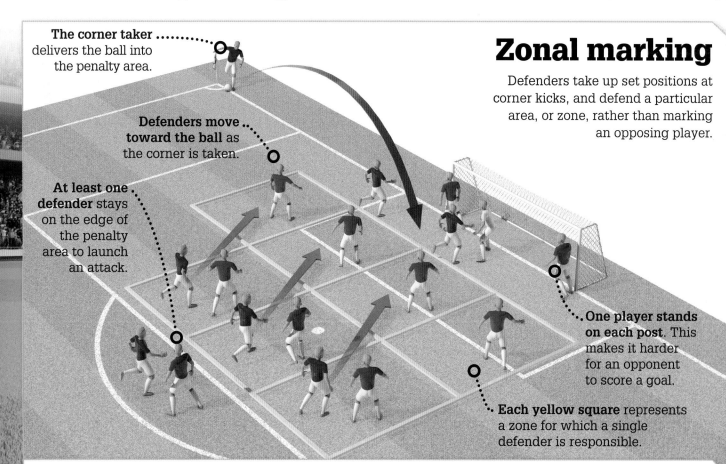

The corner taker delivers the ball into the penalty area.

Defenders move toward the ball as the corner is taken.

At least one defender stays on the edge of the penalty area to launch an attack.

Zonal marking

Defenders take up set positions at corner kicks, and defend a particular area, or zone, rather than marking an opposing player.

One player stands on each post. This makes it harder for an opponent to score a goal.

Each yellow square represents a zone for which a single defender is responsible.

✔ Advantages

- This system leaves goalkeeper free to come and collect the ball, because the area around him/her is likely to be less congested.
- Defending becomes a team responsibility.

✘ Disadvantages

- It is easier for attackers to win a header, because, as they have a further distance to run toward the ball, they can arrive at it at greater speed and leap higher.

Defensive walls for free kicks

The goalkeeper decides how many players should be in a defensive wall. That number depends on where the free kick is taken from. Each segment in this illustration shows how many players would be in a wall if a free kick is taken inside it.

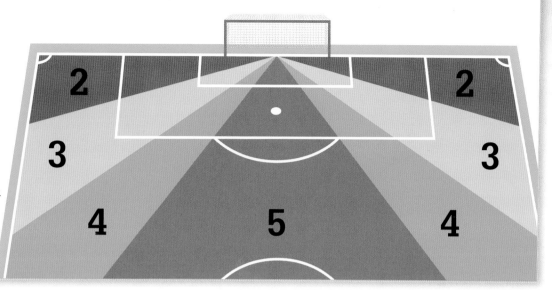

The corner taker delivers the ball into the penalty area.

Attackers will try to lose their marker to get a free run at the ball.

Man-to-man marking

Each defender picks up an opposition player, and is responsible for staying with him until the ball has been cleared and the danger is over.

One defender stands on each post, as with zonal marking.

Defenders must always stay goalside of the attacker they are marking.

✔ Advantages

- Defenders can get the same run at the ball as attackers.

✘ Disadvantages

- Defenders can get dragged around the penalty area by attackers.
- The system places great responsibility on the individual defender not to lose the attacker they are marking.
- The area around the goal mouth can become congested, making it difficult for the goalkeeper to come and claim the ball.

Soccer genius

Every team takes to the field with a **strategy** to help them win the game. This is devised by the **manager**, based on a **style of play** the team has developed over many years.

1930s

The passing method of play was introduced in 1870 by Scottish side Queen of the South. The team revolutionized the game from one that was solely based on dribbling.

1870s

Herbert Chapman founded the WM formation in the 1930s while managing English club Arsenal. The strategy focused on defense—previously the game was all about attacking.

Helenio Herrera managed Italian side Inter Milan to European Cup glory in 1964 and 1965. Using a defensive style called catenaccio, the team won games by scoring on the counterattack.

Hungary scored a record **27 goals** at the **1954 FIFA World Cup.**

1960s

The era of modern soccer has seen the emergence of many different strategies and playing styles. Here is a selection that have led to great success on the field.

1950s

Hungary played a unique formation in the 1950s, which saw the striker swap roles with midfielders, pulling opposition players out of position. The team won the Olympic gold medal in 1952.

2000s

The Netherlands team of the 1970s adopted a style of play known as Total Football, in which players swapped roles on the field. The team was a FIFA World Cup finalist in 1974 and 1978.

Pep Guardiola's reign at Spanish club Barcelona saw the side using a possession-based style called Tiki-taka to win multiple trophies between 2008–2012.

Vicente del Bosque masterminded Spain's FIFA World Cup triumph in 2010. The team used a system called the False Nine, which features no recognized striker, but a trio of attacking midfielders instead.

2010

1970s

2010s

RINUS MICHELS

Rinus Michels is credited as inventing Total Football. In 1971, he led Dutch side Ajax to the first of three successive European Cup wins. He also introduced the style of play to Spanish side Barcelona and the Netherlands team, leading the Dutch to European Championship glory in 1988.

Jurgen Klopp led German club Borussia Dortmund to league titles in 2011 and 2012. He used a strategy called Gegenpressing, in which a team moves further up the field every time it loses possession to win back the ball as quickly as possible.

Overtime

The **average** number of **goals scored per game** across the top leagues in **China, England, France, Germany, Italy, Spain,** and the **US** is **2.78**.

Spanish club **Barcelona** made a *record* **993 passes** against German side **Borussia Mönchengladbach** in a 2011 **Champions League game. Barcelona won the game 4–0**.

The **most common scoreline** in soccer games is 1—1, making up **11** percent of all results. Here are the percentages of other common scorelines.

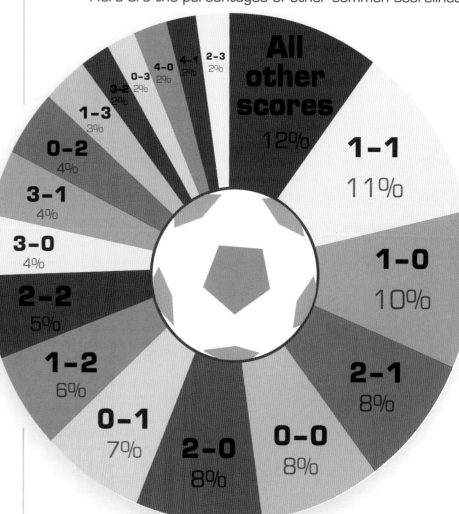

- **All other scores** 12%
- **1–1** 11%
- **1–0** 10%
- **2–1** 8%
- **0–0** 8%
- **2–0** 8%
- **0–1** 7%
- **1–2** 6%
- **2–2** 5%
- **3–0** 4%
- **3–1** 4%
- **0–2** 4%
- **1–3** 3%
- **3–2** 2%
- **0–3** 2%
- **4–0** 2%
- **4–1** 2%
- **2–3** 2%

During a **90-minute game** (excluding injury time), the **actual time the ball is in play** ranges between **60–65 minutes**. At non-professional level, the figure is between **50–55 minutes**.

A study of the English Premier League reveals **when goals** are **commonly scored** during a game.

0–15 minutes	**12.2% of goals**
16–30 minutes	**12.4% of goals**
31–45 minutes	**18.7% of goals**
46–60 minutes	**16.7% of goals**
61–75 minutes	**16.6% of goals**
76–90 minutes	**23.4% of goals**

In professional soccer, the **team that scores first** has only a **one in seven chance** of losing the game.

The longest-ever

undefeated run of games in top-level soccer are:

Celtic
(Scotland)
1915–17

62 GAMES

Union SG
(Belgium)
1933–35

60 GAMES

Benfica
(Portugal)
1963–65

48 GAMES

Dinamo Zagreb
(Croatia)
1915–17

45 GAMES

Juventus
(Italy)
2011–12

43 GAMES

On average, **9** out of every **100 shots** result in a **goal**. In contrast, **12** out of every **100 headers** on goal end up in the *back of the net*.

Dutch side Ajax won all **46 home games** for *two seasons in a row* **(1971–72 and 1972–73)**, also picking up **four titles:**

the **Dutch league title**, the KNVB Cup, the **European Cup**, and the Intercontinental Cup.

Club world

A soccer team is part of a much larger organization— the club, which has its own identity and tradition. Top clubs are run like businesses and employ hundreds of people. There are many different jobs to be done to keep a club running, from managing the team to selling tickets to fans and preparing the field for game day.

Running a club

A large soccer club **employs people** with many different skills to ensure it **succeeds on the field** and as a **business.**

This diagram shows the different people who work at a soccer club, and explains what they do and how they work together to make sure that the club runs smoothly.

English club **Notts County** is recognized as **the world's first** professional soccer club.

The directors are usually part owners of the club. They make the decisions about the club and its future plans.

COMMERCIAL DIRECTOR

The commerical director's role involves negotiating deals with sponsors and other businesses.

The manager is in charge of the first team. He or she controls training, picks the team, and sets the tactics for every game.

The chief executive officer (CEO) manages the day-to-day running of the whole club, and reports to the board of directors.

BOARD OF DIRECTORS

CEO

FIRST TEAM MANAGER

The financial director takes care of the club's funds, and makes sure the club is making a profit.

FINANCIAL DIRECTOR

TECHNICAL DIRECTOR

The technical director devises the coaching programs and is also in charge of signing new players.

The doctor provides medical care for the first team squad.

CLUB DOCTOR

PHYSIO

The physio takes care of injured players and reports to the club doctor.

FIRST TEAM

ASSISTANT MANAGER

... **manager** helps the first team manager prepare the team for every game.

COACHES

The team is picked from a total squad of 20–30 players, who provide cover for any injuries.

Coaches are responsible for the team's training. Each coach specializes in a different aspect of training.

YOUTH SOCCER DEVELOPMENT MANAGER

The youth soccer development manager is in charge of the local youth leagues.

SCOUTS

HEAD OF SALES

The head of sales oversees the sale of tickets and club merchandise.

Scouts attend other soccer games on behalf of the club and look out for talented players.

LOCAL SOCCER DEVELOPMENT OFFICER

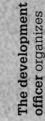

The development officer organizes and delivers a range of soccer activities for the local community.

The manager

Managers have to juggle **many tasks.** They are responsible for every aspect of **every team at a club,** from youth team to the first XI, and must also **speak to journalists.**

Guy Roux managed French club **Auxerre for 44 years** (1961–2004).

In the spotlight

- Dealing with the media.
- Preparing program notes.
- Helping club sponsors.
- Attending club events.
- Appearing on the club's TV channel.

Team and players

- Deciding on formations.
- Selecting the team.
- Motivating the players.
- Giving team talks during the game.
- Making substitutions.

Behind the scenes

- Maintaining player discipline.
- Running the club.
- Overseeing player development.
- Setting coaching policy.

Running the club

- Buying and selling players.
- Appointing coaching staff.
- Overseeing coaching activities.
- Attending board meetings.
- Scouting for new players.

MANAGERIAL MERRY-GO-ROUND

England — 11
Italy — 21
Spain — 16
France — 11
Germany — 11

The job of a top-flight soccer manager is among the least secure in the world. This chart shows the average number of managerial changes each year in Europe's top-five leagues.

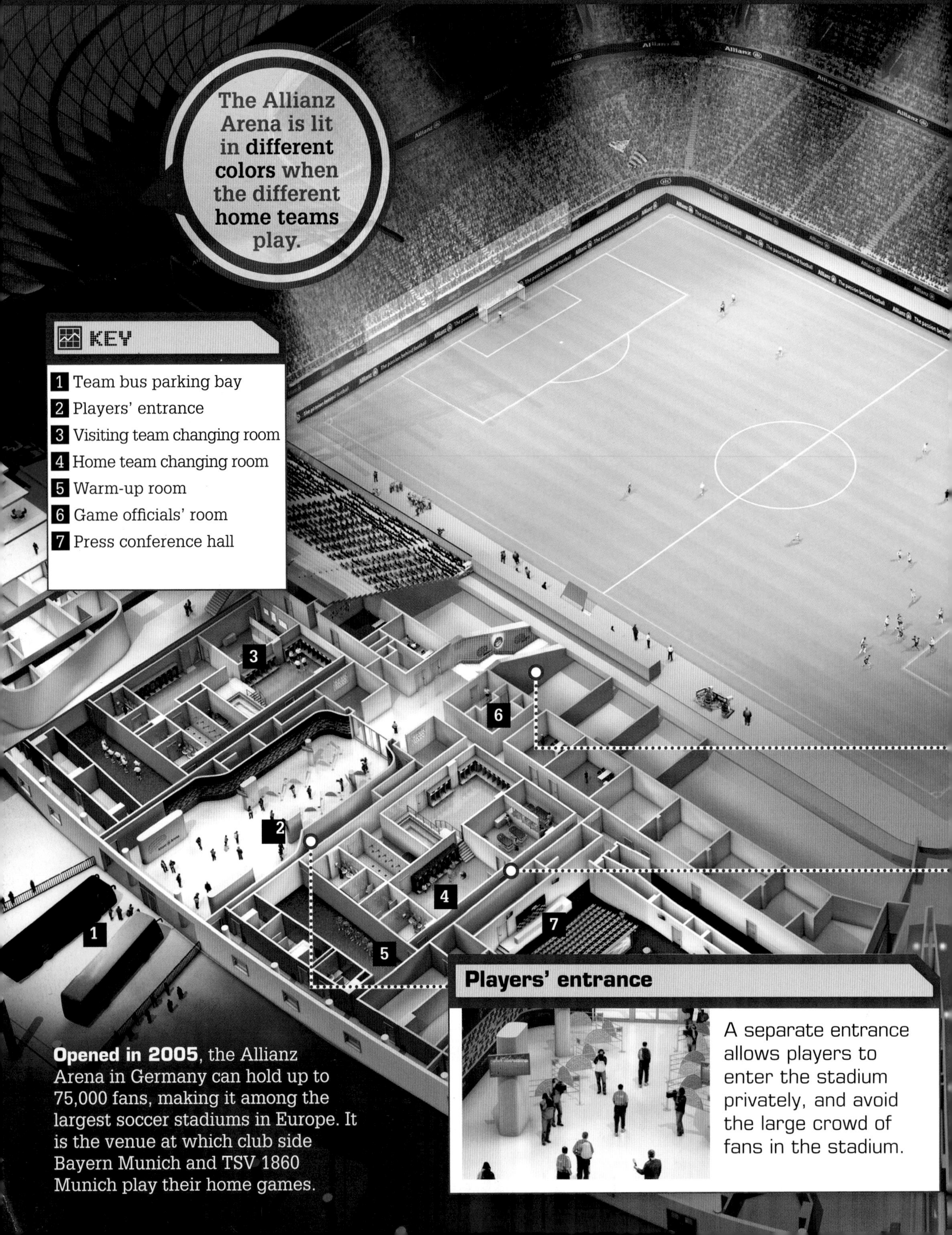

The Allianz Arena is lit in **different colors** when the different home teams play.

KEY

1 Team bus parking bay
2 Players' entrance
3 Visiting team changing room
4 Home team changing room
5 Warm-up room
6 Game officials' room
7 Press conference hall

Opened in 2005, the Allianz Arena in Germany can hold up to 75,000 fans, making it among the largest soccer stadiums in Europe. It is the venue at which club side Bayern Munich and TSV 1860 Munich play their home games.

Players' entrance

A separate entrance allows players to enter the stadium privately, and avoid the large crowd of fans in the stadium.

The stadium

A team's stadium features a field surrounded by **thousands of seats** for fans who come to watch the matches. It also includes all the **facilities** players need to prepare for a game.

Locker room

The locker room is where players change into their kit and gather for the captain's final team talk.

The tunnel

The players' tunnel leads on to the field. Players of both teams line up in the tunnel before the game.

Transfers

Professional soccer has two **transfer windows**: the first runs from July to September, and the second is in January. They are an exciting time for soccer fans, but **how do transfers actually work?**

A scout's job is to find talented new players. Larger clubs may have as many as 15 scouts.

Player scouted

Finding the right player is only the start of a long process. A club has to go through many stages before a player officially signs for them.

The bid

Agent talks

Once a club has found a player it wants, it will make a bid to the club the player currently plays for. Normally, it takes several bids before one is accepted.

After the bid has been accepted, a club starts contract talks with a player's agent. The two parties must agree on details such as wages and performance-related bonuses.

WORTH HIS WEIGHT IN GOLD

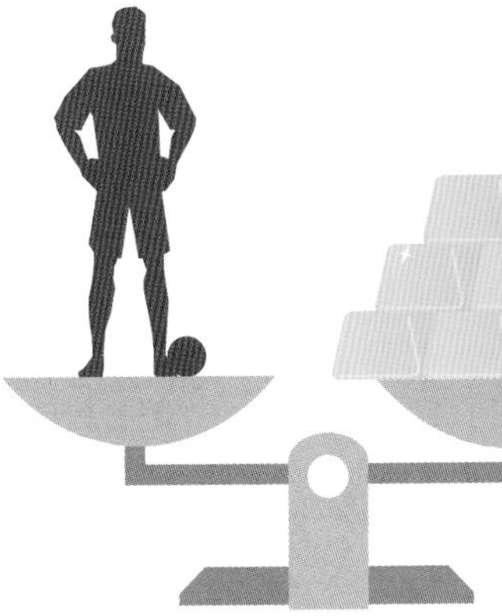

The first player who was literally worth his weight in gold was Bernabé Ferreryra. Argentine club River Plate paid $45,000 for his services in 1932, comfortably more money than his equivalent weight in gold at the time.

An agent's commission is usually **5 percent** of the transfer fee.

Finalizing contracts

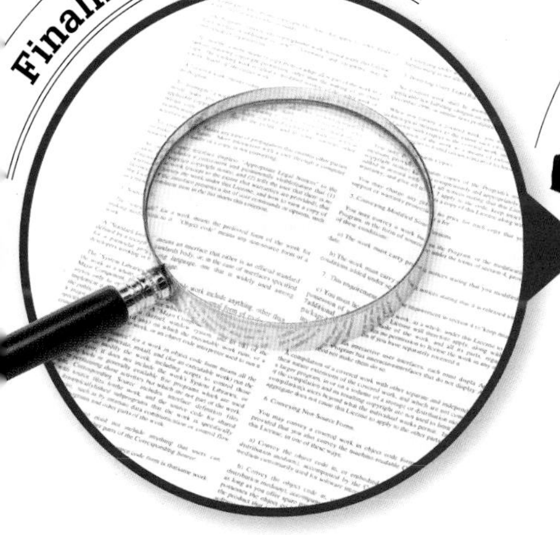

The player and the buying club must agree on every detail in the contract. One Premier League player had a clause in his contract that prevented him from traveling to space!

The medical

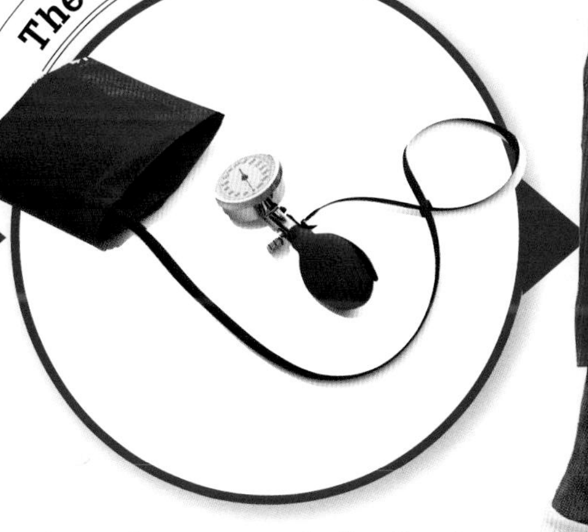

Once the contract is finalized, a player then has to take a thorough medical examination to confirm fitness. This identifies any hidden injuries or weaknesses.

Done deal

Once the player has passed the medical, the deal is officially done.

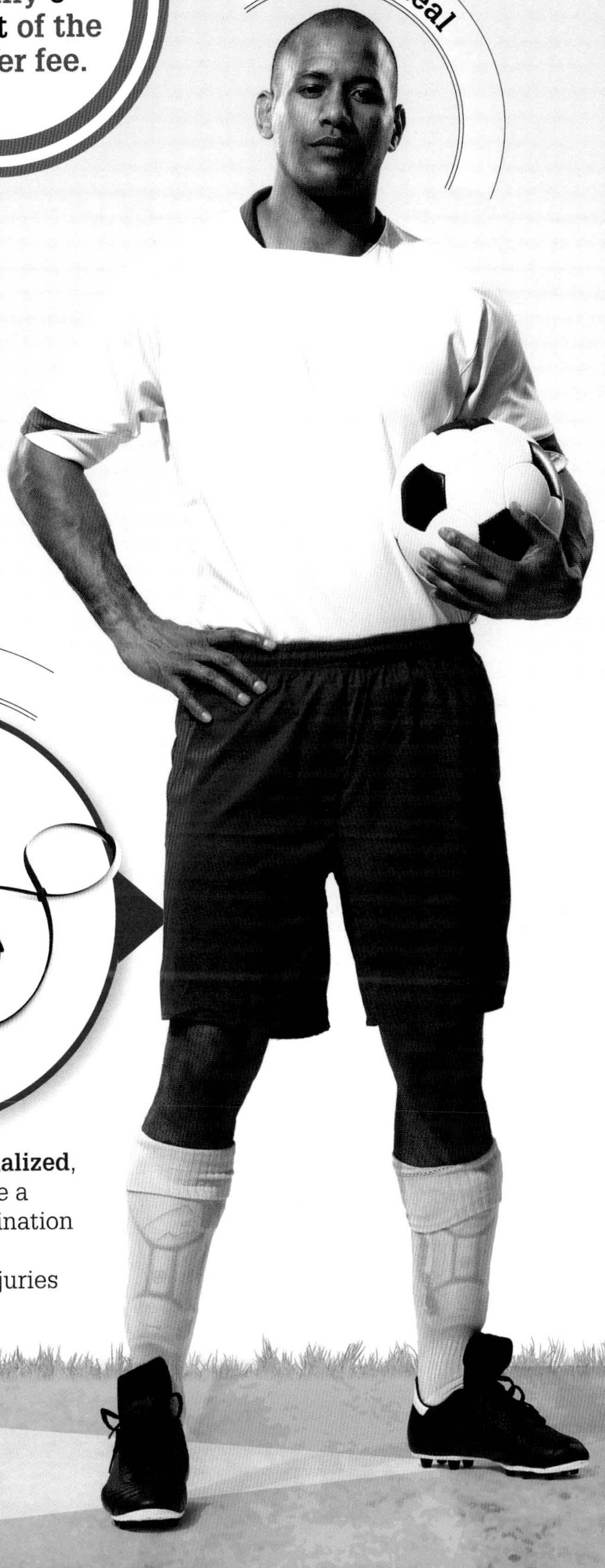

Training

Players mainly **practice** their **ball skills** during training, but also work on their **speed** and **agility**, **stamina**, **strength**, and **tactical awareness**.

Speed and agility

High-intensity exercises, such as sprints around obstacles, shuttle runs, hurdle hopping, and squat jumps, all help to improve a player's speed and agility.

📊 FAST FACTS

Soccer	7–9.5 miles (11–15 km)
Rugby	4–7 miles (6.5 –11 km)
Hockey	4–5 miles (6.5–8 km)
Tennis	3–5 miles (5–8 km)
Basketball	2–3 miles (3–5 km)
Football	1.25 miles (2 km)

Soccer players are exceptionally fit. They typically cover a distance of between 7–9.5 miles (11–15 km) during a 90-minute game.

Ball skills

Players regularly train their ball skills. The also play practice games in which they work on set pieces and different modes of attack and defense.

Professional players spend an **average of three hours** a day training.

During training, players shed between 2 to 3 lbs (1–1.5 kg) of weight through sweat loss. The amount can rise to 6.5 lbs (3 kg) during a game played on a hot day. To stay hydrated, experts recommend that players consume about 40–50 fl oz (1.2–1.5 liters) of fluid for each 2.2 lbs (1 kg) of weight they lose.

Stamina

The team performs stamina-building exercises such as running and circuit drills. All players must be fit enough to play a full game without tiring.

Strength

Gym workouts are specially devised to develop players' leg muscles and overall body strength.

Tactical awareness

The coach works with the players to make sure they know their roles and can follow the game plan during the high-pressure situation of a game.

Injury time

Soccer is a physical game in **which** players have to **sprint, jump, twist, turn,** and **tackle.** These actions place huge stress on the **muscles, joints,** and **bones,** and can sometimes cause **injuries.**

The red circles highlight the parts of the body that players are most likely to injure in a game. The number inside each circle refers to the number of injuries suffered in that area of the body out of every 100 injuries.

Concussion
Head injury resulting from a collision with another player.

Shoulder dislocation
Dislodged shoulder bone caused by an awkward fall.

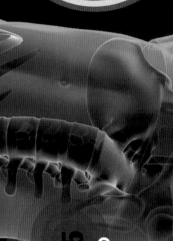

Professional players sustain an average of **two injuries** per season.

Back strain
Muscle sprain or tear from overstretching the spine.

Broken finger
An injury suffered mostly by goalkeepers.

Dead leg
Severe bruising of the muscle resulting from a hard blow.

Shin splints
Tiny fractures caused by constant impact.

14

11

14

Groin strain
Overstretching of the groin muscle, caused by overreaching for the ball.

Hamstring strain
Muscle sprain caused by sprinting to chase the ball.

Calf strain
Muscle sprain or tear from overstretching the lower leg.

Twisted ankle
Severe sprain caused by turning too rapidly or a bad tackle.

23

18

Thigh strain
Tear or spraining of the thigh muscle, caused by overuse.

Knee ligament damage
Overbending of the knee joint, usually caused by a reckless tackle.

Achilles strain
Strained tendon in heel resulting from overuse.

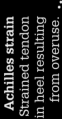

Metatarsal fracture
Cracked foot bone usually caused from a tackle with raised studs.

6

The physio's role

The physio treats players who get injured during a game and helps with their recovery afterward. The physio also assesses the fitness of players, and helps to devise individual training programs that ensure that the players stay fit throughout the season.

A player's week

Most professional soccer players lead very **disciplined lives**. They follow a **strict routine** to ensure that they are **fully prepared** for a game. This includes getting as much **rest** as possible between games.

ICE BATHS

After every game, players take ice baths to treat muscle soreness. The cold makes the blood vessels tighten, draining out the blood. This allows oxygen-rich blood to get into the muscles and helps speed up recovery.

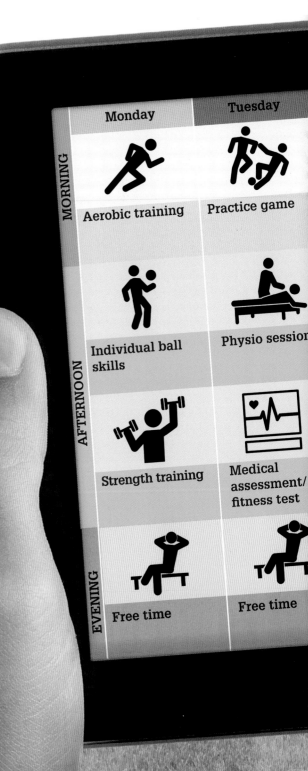

	Monday	Tuesday
MORNING	Aerobic training	Practice game
AFTERNOON	Individual ball skills	Physio session
	Strength training	Medical assessment/ fitness test
EVENING	Free time	Free time

Below is an example of a professional player's weekly schedule. It reveals just how much training is involved. Recovery time is equally important—players need about 8–10 hours of sleep a night.

Professional soccer players spend about **15 hours** a week training with the ball.

...dnesday	Thursday	Friday	Saturday	Sunday
...ctical ...eparation	Recovery—light and low impact workout	Power and speed training session	Group ball skills	Recovery—light and low impact workout
...etching—...us on ...xibility	Post-game debrief led by the manager	Practice game	Travel to away game on team bus	Post-game debrief led by the manager
...oup ...ll skills	Individual ball skills	Tactical preparation	AWAY GAME K.O: 3:00pm	Physio session
...OME GAME: ...O: 7:45pm	Free time	Free time	Travel back from away game	Free time

The fans

True **soccer fans** are not just spectators, but eager participants who think of themselves as the team's **"twelfth" player**. They **chant**, **sing**, and voice their **opinions**, creating the **lively atmosphere** that spurs the team on.

Replica jerseys, hats, and scarves bearing the team's colors are worn to the game.

Eight out of 10 fans believe that their **support** helps the team to play better.

Fans revel in the loud and energetic atmosphere they create in the stadium. Some look forward to being around fellow fans as much as watching the game itself.

FAST FACTS

Soccer has a global fanbase of about 3.5 billion, which is more than any other sport in the world. About 64 percent of these fans are male and 36 percent are female.

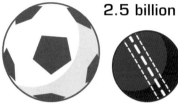
3.5 billion
Soccer

2.5 billion
Cricket

2.2 billion
Basketball

2 billion
Tennis

1 billion
Volleyball

0.9 billion
Field hockey

Die-hard fans often use the melody of popular songs to make up catchy chants.

Some fans wave flags to show their support.

FAN POWER

The general trend across world soccer reveals that home teams win half of their games and lose just one in four. This might be down to the atmosphere home fans create, giving their side a mental edge against the visiting team.

Overtime

The soccer clubs with the **highest number** of **fans** worldwide are:

1
Manchester United
(England)
670 million
fans

2
Barcelona
(Spain)
290 million
fans

3
Real Madrid
(Spain)
195 million
fans

4
Chelsea
(England)
145 million
fans

5
Arsenal
(England)
125 million
fans

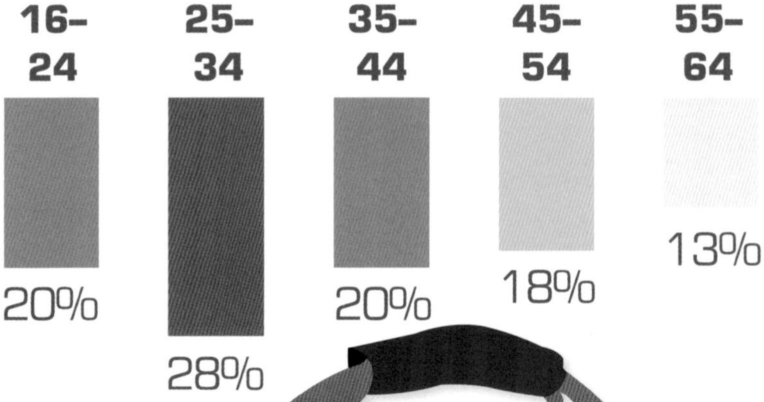

77 **percent** of **European fans** have **traveled abroad** to watch a game. **England** is the most **popular country** for fans to visit to watch a soccer game, followed by **Spain**.

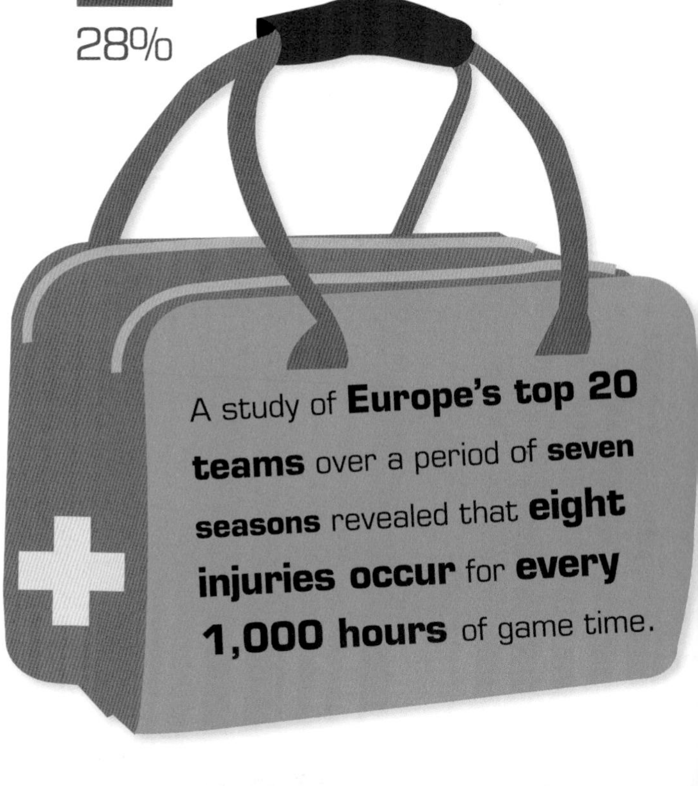

Europe's **longest-serving soccer managers** are:

5	**Vittori Pozzo:** 21 yrs (1929–48) at Italy (National team)	
4	**Alex Ferguson:** 27 yrs (1986–2013) at Manchester United (England)	
3	**Bill Struth:** 34 yrs (1921–1954) at Rangers (Scotland)	
2	**Willie Maley:** 43 yrs (1897–1940) at Celtic (Scotland)	
1	**Guy Roux:** 44 yrs (1961–2005) at Auxerre (France)	

How old are soccer fans?

The chart shows the **percentage** of all soccer fans in five different age groups.

16–24	25–34	35–44	45–54	55–64
20%	28%	20%	18%	13%

A study of **Europe's top 20 teams** over a period of **seven seasons** revealed that **eight injuries occur** for **every 1,000 hours** of game time.

The **non-European clubs** with the **highest average attendances** are:

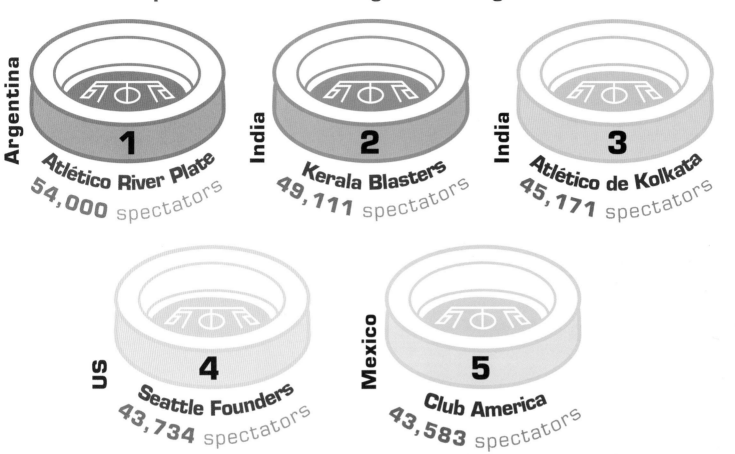

Argentina

1

Atlético River Plate
54,000 spectators

India

2

Kerala Blasters
49,111 spectators

India

3

Atlético de Kolkata
45,171 spectators

US

4

Seattle Founders
43,734 spectators

Mexico

5

Club America
43,583 spectators

The 1950 FIFA World Cup game between **Uruguay** and **Brazil** at the **Maracana Stadium** recorded the **highest-ever** attendance:

199,854.

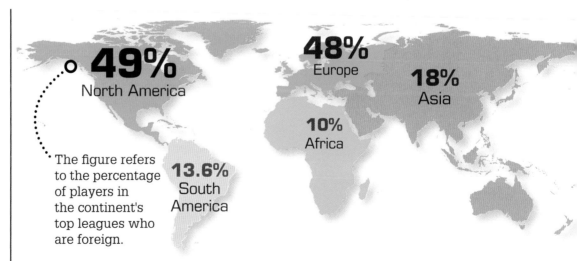

49%
North America

The figure refers to the percentage of players in the continent's top leagues who are foreign.

13.6%
South America

48%
Europe

18%
Asia

10%
Africa

Foreign players in high demand

Almost half of the professional players signed to the top clubs in **North America** and **Europe** are foreign. These clubs are among the richest and attract the world's best players.

Tournaments and trophies

The success of a team is measured by the number of tournaments and trophies it has won. At international level, national teams play for the FIFA World Cup every four years. In addition, every continent has its own competition to determine its continental champion.

FIFA World Cup

Played for the first time in 1930, and staged every four years, the FIFA World Cup is the **biggest competition** in soccer. It decides who becomes the game's **world champion team**.

Diego Maradona confirmed **his status as the world's best player** when he led Argentina to a 3–2 victory over West Germany in the 1986 FIFA World Cup final in the Azteca Stadium, Mexico City.

1970: Brilliant Brazil
Brazil beat Italy 4–1 in the final in Mexico City. This was the first time two former champions had met in the final. It was also the first time a FIFA World Cup tournament was screened in color.

1982: Inspired Italy
Goals from Paolo Rossi, Marco Tardelli (both above), and Alessandro Altobelli helped Italy to a 3–1 victory over West Germany in a gripping final. Victory saw Italy join Brazil as three-time FIFA World Cup winners.

Only 13 teams contested the first FIFA World Cup in Uruguay in 1930.

COMPETITION FACTS

First played:
1930

Confederation:
FIFA

Number of teams:
32

Qualifying to determine the 32-team line-up for the FIFA World Cup usually starts three years before the start of the tournament.

UEFA European Championship

The UEFA European Championship was **first played in 1960** and is staged every four years. It determines the **champion of Europe**.

Despite being called up to play in the tournament as a last-minute replacement, Denmark shocked Germany 2–0 in the 1992 final.

📈 COMPETITION FACTS

First played:
1960

Confederation:
UEFA

Number of teams:
24

The number of qualifying teams for the UEFA European Championship finals was increased to 24 for the first time in 2016.

Spain and **Germany** have both won the tournament on **three** occasions.

TOURNAMENT HIGHLIGHTS

1984: Allez les Bleus
Michel Platini (above) led France to victory on home soil by scoring nine goals in the tournament (a record), including one in France's 2–0 final victory over Spain.

1988: Beautiful orange
Goals from Ruud Gullit and Marco van Basten helped the Netherlands beat the Soviet Union 2–0 in the final. This is the Netherlands' only international tournament victory.

2012: Spanish double
Two goals in each half saw Spain demolish Italy 4–0 in the final to become the first team in the tournament's history to defend their title successfully.

Copa América

The Copa América is the **world's oldest** international soccer tournament. First staged in 1916 and **held every four years**, it determines the **champion of South America**.

Goalkeeper Claudio Bravo was Chile's hero in the 2016 tournament when he helped his side beat Argentina on penalties. It was the second time Chile had won the tournament.

COMPETITION FACTS

First played:
1916

Confederation:
CONMEBOL

Number of teams:
12

The current format features 12 teams. There is a group stage (three groups of four teams) that is followed by a knockout stage.

TOURNAMENT HIGHLIGHTS

1949: Brazil end 27-year wait
Zizinho (above right) led Brazil as they crushed Paraguay 7–0 in the final. It was Brazil's third Copa América success, but the first time they had won the tournament for 27 years.

1979: Perfect Paraguay
Paraguay beat Chile 3–1 on aggregate in the final (they won 3–0 in the first leg before losing 1–0 in the second) to win the trophy for the second time.

1993: Beyond the boundaries
Argentina beat Mexico 2–1 in the final. This was the first time teams from outside South America (Mexico and the United States) had competed in the tournament.

Brazil and Uruguay have won the tournament every time they have been hosts.

Africa Cup of Nations

Only **three countries** took part in the first-ever Africa Cup of Nations in 1957.

📈 COMPETITION FACTS

First played:
1957

Confederation:
CAF

Number of teams:
16

Qualifying for the tournament sees 52 teams split into 13 groups. The group winners, plus the two best runners-up, qualify for the finals.

The **Africa Cup of Nations** is a tournament to decide the **champions of Africa**. It was held for the first time in 1957 and, unlike most other major tournaments, is **staged every two years**.

Having lost the 2006 and 2012 finals on penalties, the Ivory Coast finally ended up on the right side of the penalty shootout lottery when they beat Ghana 9–8 on penalties in the 2015 final.

TOURNAMENT HIGHLIGHTS

1988: Classy Cameroon
Cameroon, led by Roger Milla (above), confirmed their status as Africa's dominant team when they beat Nigeria 1–0 in the final. It was their second title in four years.

1996: Home comforts
Two goals from Mark Williams saw South Africa mark their first appearance in the tournament by beating Tunisia 2–0 in the final in Johannesburg.

2008: Egypt's sensational six
Egypt beat Cameroon 1–0 in the final to win the tournament for the sixth time—a seventh tournament victory followed in 2010.

TOURNAMENT HIGHLIGHTS

1996: Super Saudi
Goalkeeper Mohamed-Al-Deayea (above) helped Saudi Arabia beat the United Arab Emirates 4–2 on penalties in the final, to win the tournament for the third time.

2007: Jakarta joy for Iraq
Iraq put the political turmoil in their own country to one side when they beat Saudi Arabia 1–0 in the final in Jakarta, Indonesia, to win the tournament for the first time.

2011: Fourth title for Japan
A 109th-minute goal from Tadanari Lee saw Japan beat Australia 1–0 in the final in Doha, Qatar, to win the AFC Asian Cup for a record fourth time.

Hosts Australia, runners-up in 2011, beat South Korea 2–1 in overtime in the 2015 final in Sydney to win the tournament for the first time.

Australia joined the Asian confederation in 2007 and won the tournament in 2015.

AFC Asia Cup

First contested in 1956, the **AFC Asian Cup** is the **second oldest** continental soccer championship in the world, after the Copa América. It is **staged every four years.**

COMPETITION FACTS

First played:
1956

Confederation:
AFC

Number of teams:
16

Ten teams from five qualifying groups join the teams that finished first, second, and third in the previous tournament, plus the hosts.

Olympic Games

Men's soccer was included on the Olympic Games program for the **first time in 1900**. **Women** had to wait until **1996** before they had their own tournament.

COMPETITION FACTS

First played:
1900 (men);
1996 (women)

Number of teams:
16 (men);
12 (women)

The winners of continental age-group tournaments qualify for the men's competition. Women's teams qualify via numerous continental qualifying tournaments.

Soccer has been played at every summer Olympic Games except 1896 and 1932.

After collecting silver medals in 1984, 1988, and 2012, Brazil finally struck gold at their home Olympic Games in Rio de Janeiro in 2016. They beat Germany 5–4 on penalties in the final.

TOURNAMENT HIGHLIGHTS

1952: Mighty Magyars
Hungary, known as the Mighty Magyars, confirmed their status as the best team in world soccer when they beat Yugoslavia 2–0 in the final in Helsinki, Finland.

1996: Olympic firsts
The United States won the inaugural women's tournament at the Olympic Games. Nigeria became the first team from Africa to win men's Olympic gold.

2000: Norway strikes gold
Norway beat reigning champions the United States 3–2 in the women's Olympic final — the only final in Olympic history to be won by an overtime golden goal.

FIFA Women's World Cup

The **FIFA Women's World Cup** was held for the **first time in 1991**. A 24-team competition, it is **staged every four years**, and is growing in size, recognition, and status.

The United States beat defending champions Japan 5–2 in the 2015 final, to win the tournament for a record third time.

An unofficial Women's World Cup, won by Denmark, was held in Italy in 1970.

COMPETITION FACTS

First played:
1991

Confederation:
FIFA

Number of teams:
24

Qualifying tournaments are staged in each confederation to determine the 24 teams that qualify for the Women's FIFA World Cup finals.

TOURNAMENT HIGHLIGHTS

1991: First champions
Two goals from Michelle Akers saw the United States beat Norway 2–1 to win the first-ever FIFA Women's World Cup final, staged in Guangzhou, China.

2007: Double gold for Germany
Germany became the first team to defend their world crown as goals from Birgit Prinz and Simone Laudehr helped them to a 2–0 victory over Brazil in the final.

2011: Japan's joy
Japan became the first world champion team from Asia after they beat the United States 3–1 on penalties in the final in Frankfurt, Germany.

TOURNAMENT HIGHLIGHTS

1960: Magnificent Madrid

Alfredo Di Stéfano (three goals) and Ferenc Puskás (two) starred as Real Madrid beat Eintracht Frankfurt 7–3 in the final to record a fifth-successive triumph.

1973: Dutch masters

Ajax beat Juventus 1–0 in the final in Belgrade, Serbia, to become the first team since Real Madrid to win three finals in a row.

1981: Mighty Reds

Liverpool lifted the cup for the third time in five years, beating Real Madrid 1–0 in the final in Paris. Liverpool would triumph again in 1984 and 2005.

A record **360 million viewers** tuned in to watch the 2012–13 final on television.

UEFA Champions League

First staged in 1956 and known as the European Cup until 1992, the UEFA Champions League is considered the world's **most important club competition.**

Cristiano Ronaldo (left) celebrates as Real Madrid beat Atlético Madrid 4–1 in overtime in the 2014 final to claim a record tenth title. This was the first time in the tournament's history that two clubs from the same city contested the final.

COMPETITION FACTS

First played:
1956

Confederation:
UEFA

Number of teams:
78

The top teams from UEFA-qualified countries' domestic leagues qualify for the tournament. The main tournament comprises a 32-team group stage followed by a knockout phase.

Copa Libertadores

Staged for the first time in 1960 and contested annually, the **Copa Libertadores** is a competition to decide the **top club of South America**.

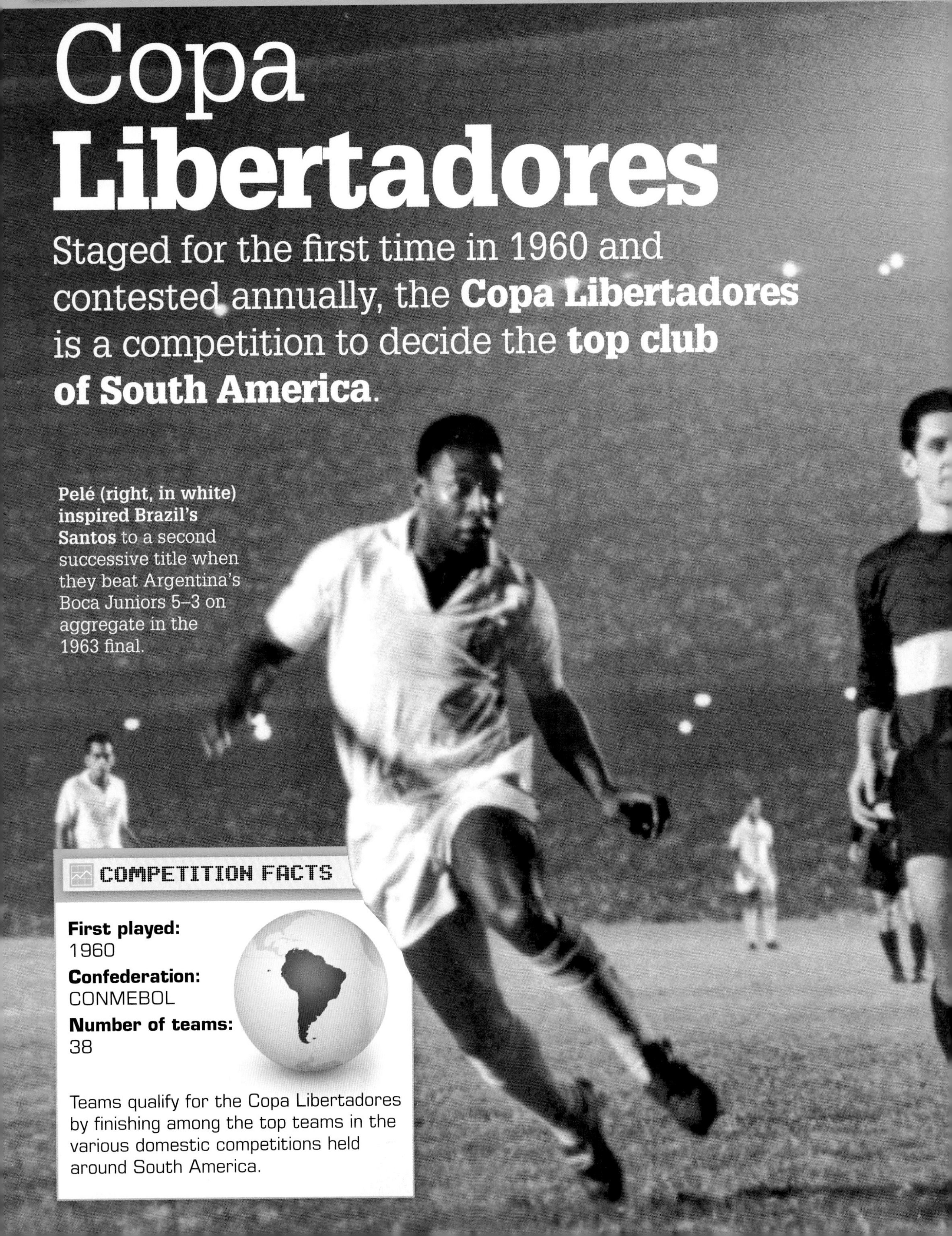

Pelé (right, in white) inspired Brazil's Santos to a second successive title when they beat Argentina's Boca Juniors 5–3 on aggregate in the 1963 final.

COMPETITION FACTS

First played:
1960

Confederation:
CONMEBOL

Number of teams:
38

Teams qualify for the Copa Libertadores by finishing among the top teams in the various domestic competitions held around South America.

1996: River Plate at the double
River Plate overturned a 1—0 first-leg deficit to beat Colombia's América 2—1 on aggregate in the final. It was their second title.

2005: Battle of Brazil
São Paulo beat Atlético Paranaense 5—1 on aggregate in the final. This was the first-ever final contested by two teams from Brazil.

2007: Dominant force
Argentina's Boca Juniors reached the final for the fifth time in eight years and beat Brazil's Grêmio 5—0 on aggregate.

Argentine
Carlos Bianchi
is the only
manager to
win the trophy
four times.

Roll of honor

WINNERS

- 1930: Uruguay
- 1934: Italy
- 1938: Italy
- 1950: Uruguay
- 1954: West Germany
- 1958: Brazil
- 1962: Brazil
- 1966: England
- 1970: Brazil
- 1974: West Germany
- 1978: Argentina
- 1982: Italy
- 1986: Argentina
- 1990: West Germany
- 1994: Brazil
- 1998: France
- 2002: Brazil
- 2006: Italy
- 2010: Spain
- 2014: Germany

MOST GOALS SCORED IN A GAME

5—Oleg Salenko
Russia v Cameroon, **1994**

MOST TOURNAMENT WINS

 Brazil—5
(1958,1962,1970, 1994, 2002)

 Germany—4
(1954,1974, 1990,2014)

 Italy—4
(1934,1938, 1982, 2006)

 Uruguay—2
(1934,1950)

 Argentina—2
(1978,1986)

 England—1
(1966)

 France—1
(1998)

 Spain—1
(2010)

MOST GOALS SCORED IN A FINAL

3
Geoff Hurst

England v West Germany, 1966

MOST GOALS IN A TOURNAMENT

- **Just Fontaine—13** (France, 1958)
- **Sandor Kocsis—11** (Hungary, 1954)
- **Gerd Müller—10** (West Germany, 1970)
- **Eusebio—9** (Portugal, 1966)
- **Guillermo Stábile—8** (Uruguay, 1930)
- **Ronaldo—8** (Brazil, 2002)

UEFA EUROPEAN CHAMPIONSHIP

WINNERS

- 🏆 **1960**: Soviet Union
- 🏆 **1964**: Spain
- 🏆 **1968**: Italy
- 🏆 **1972**: West Germany
- 🏆 **1976**: Czechoslovakia
- 🏆 **1980**: West Germany
- 🏆 **1984**: France
- 🏆 **1988**: Netherlands
- 🏆 **1992**: Denmark
- 🏆 **1996**: Germany
- 🏆 **2000**: France
- 🏆 **2004**: Greece
- 🏆 **2008**: Spain
- 🏆 **2012**: Spain
- 🏆 **2016**: Portugal

MOST GOALS
IN A TOURNAMENT

- ⚽ **Michel Platini—9** (France, 1984)
- ⚽ **Antoine Griezmann—6** (France, 2016)
- ⚽ **Marco van Basten—5** (Netherlands, 1988)
- ⚽ **Alan Shearer—5** (England, 1996)
- ⚽ **Patrick Kluivert—5** (Netherlands, 2000)
- ⚽ **Savo Milosevic—5** (Yugoslavia, 2000)
- ⚽ **Milan Baros—5** (Czech Republic, 2004)

Fastest **hat trick**

18
minutes

Michel Platini
(France)

scored in the **59th**, **62nd**, and **77th** minutes v Yugoslavia in **1984**

COPA AMÉRICA

WINNERS

- 🏆 **1916**: Uruguay
- 🏆 **1917**: Uruguay
- 🏆 **1919**: Brazil
- 🏆 **1920**: Uruguay
- 🏆 **1921**: Argentina
- 🏆 **1922**: Brazil
- 🏆 **1923**: Uruguay
- 🏆 **1924**: Uruguay
- 🏆 **1925**: Argentina
- 🏆 **1926**: Uruguay
- 🏆 **1927**: Argentina
- 🏆 **1929**: Argentina
- 🏆 **1935**: Uruguay
- 🏆 **1937**: Argentina
- 🏆 **1939**: Peru
- 🏆 **1941**: Argentina
- 🏆 **1942**: Uruguay
- 🏆 **1945**: Argentina
- 🏆 **1946**: Argentina
- 🏆 **1947**: Argentina
- 🏆 **1949**: Brazil
- 🏆 **1953**: Paraguay
- 🏆 **1955**: Argentina
- 🏆 **1956**: Uruguay
- 🏆 **1957**: Argentina
- 🏆 **1959**: Argentina
- 🏆 **1959**: Uruguay*
- 🏆 **1963**: Bolivia
- 🏆 **1967**: Uruguay
- 🏆 **1975**: Peru
- 🏆 **1979**: Paraguay
- 🏆 **1983**: Uruguay
- 🏆 **1987**: Uruguay
- 🏆 **1989**: Brazil
- 🏆 **1991**: Argentina
- 🏆 **1993**: Argentina
- 🏆 **1995**: Uruguay
- 🏆 **1997**: Brazil
- 🏆 **1999**: Brazil
- 🏆 **2001**: Colombia
- 🏆 **2004**: Brazil
- 🏆 **2007**: Brazil
- 🏆 **2011**: Uruguay
- 🏆 **2015**: Chile
- 🏆 **2016**: Chile

An extra tournament was held in 1959

MOST WINS
AS A MANAGER

6

Guillermo Stábilo
(Argentina)

1941, 1945, 1946, 1947, 1955, 1957

MOST TOURNAMENT
WINS

 **Uruguay**
15

Argentina
14

 **Brazil**
8

AFRICA CUP OF NATIONS

WINNERS
🏆 **1957**: Egypt
🏆 **1959**: Egypt
🏆 **1962**: Ethiopia
🏆 **1963**: Ghana
🏆 **1965**: Ghana
🏆 **1968**: Congo-Kinshasa
🏆 **1970**: Sudan
🏆 **1972**: Congo
🏆 **1974**: Zaire
🏆 **1976**: Morocco
🏆 **1978**: Ghana
🏆 **1980**: Nigeria
🏆 **1982**: Ghana
🏆 **1984**: Cameroon
🏆 **1986**: Egypt
🏆 **1988**: Cameroon
🏆 **1990**: Algeria
🏆 **1992**: Ivory Coast
🏆 **1994**: Nigeria
🏆 **1996**: South Africa
🏆 **1998**: Egypt
🏆 **2000**: Cameroon
🏆 **2002**: Cameroon
🏆 **2004**: Tunisia
🏆 **2006**: Egypt
🏆 **2008**: Egypt
🏆 **2010**: Egypt
🏆 **2012**: Zambia
🏆 **2013**: Nigeria
🏆 **2015**: Ivory Coast
🏆 **2017**: Cameroon

MOST GOALS IN A TOURNAMENT

⚽ **Ndaye Mulamba—9** (DR Congo, 1974)
⚽ **Laurent Pokou—8** (Ivory Coast, 1970)
⚽ **Hossam Hassan—7** (Egypt, 1998)
⚽ **Benny McCarthy—7** (South Africa, 1998)
⚽ **Laurent Pokou—6** (Ivory Coast, 1968)
⚽ **Hassan El-Shazly—6** (Egypt, 1963)

AFC ASIA CUP

WINNERS
🏆 **1956**: South Korea
🏆 **1960**: South Korea
🏆 **1964**: Israel
🏆 **1968**: Iran
🏆 **1972**: Iran
🏆 **1976**: Iran
🏆 **1980**: Kuwait
🏆 **1984**: Saudi Arabia
🏆 **1988**: Saudi Arabia
🏆 **1992**: Japan
🏆 **1996**: Saudi Arabia
🏆 **2000**: Japan
🏆 **2004**: Japan
🏆 **2007**: Iraq
🏆 **2011**: Japan
🏆 **2015**: Australia

MOST TOURNAMENT WINS
 Japan 4
 Iran 3
 Saudi Arabia 3

OLYMPIC GAMES

WINNERS

- 🏆 **1900**: Great Britain
- 🏆 **1904**: Canada
- 🏆 **1908**: Great Britain
- 🏆 **1912**: Great Britain
- 🏆 **1920**: Belgium
- 🏆 **1924**: Uruguay
- 🏆 **1928**: Uruguay
- 🏆 **1932**: *No tournament*
- 🏆 **1936**: Italy
- 🏆 **1948**: Sweden
- 🏆 **1952**: Hungary
- 🏆 **1956**: Soviet Union
- 🏆 **1960**: Yugoslavia
- 🏆 **1964**: Hungary
- 🏆 **1968**: Hungary
- 🏆 **1972**: Poland
- 🏆 **1976**: East Germany
- 🏆 **1980**: Czechoslovakia
- 🏆 **1984**: France
- 🏆 **1988**: Soviet Union
- 🏆 **1992**: Spain
- 🏆 **1996**: Nigeria (men); United States (women)
- 🏆 **2000**: Cameroon (men); Norway (women)
- 🏆 **2004**: Argentina (men); United States (women)
- 🏆 **2008**: Argentina (men); United States (women)
- 🏆 **2012**: Mexico (men); United States (women)
- 🏆 **2016**: Brazil (men); Germany (women)

WOMEN: MOST TOURNAMENT WINS

 United States—4
 Norway—1
Germany—1

WOMEN: MOST GOALS IN A TOURNAMENT

- **Christine Sinclair—6** (Canada, 2012)
- **Cristiane—5** (Brazil, 2004 and 2008)
- **Birgit Prinz—5** (Germany, 2004)
- **Melanie Behringer—5** (Germany, 2016)

MEN: MOST TOURNAMENT WINS

Great Britain 3

Argentina 2

Hungary 3

Soviet Union 2

WINNERS

- 🏆 **1991**: United States
- 🏆 **1995**: Norway
- 🏆 **1999**: United States
- 🏆 **2003**: Germany
- 🏆 **2007**: Germany
- 🏆 **2011**: Japan
- 🏆 **2015**: United States

MOST GOALS IN A TOURNAMENT

- **Michelle Akers—10** (United States, 1991)
- **Heidi Mohr—7** (Germany, 1991)
- **Sissi—7** (Brazil, 1999)
- **Sun Wen—7** (China, 1999)
- **Birgit Prinz—7** (Germany, 2003)

MOST TOURNAMENT WINS

 United States 3

 Norway 1

Germany 2

 **Japan** 1

WINNERS

- 🏆 **1956**: Real Madrid
- 🏆 **1957**: Real Madrid
- 🏆 **1958**: Real Madrid
- 🏆 **1959**: Real Madrid
- 🏆 **1960**: Real Madrid
- 🏆 **1961**: Benfica
- 🏆 **1962**: Benfica
- 🏆 **1963**: Milan
- 🏆 **1964**: Internazionale
- 🏆 **1965**: Internazionale
- 🏆 **1966**: Real Madrid
- 🏆 **1967**: Celtic
- 🏆 **1968**: Manchester United
- 🏆 **1969**: Milan
- 🏆 **1970**: Feyenoord
- 🏆 **1971**: Ajax
- 🏆 **1972**: Ajax
- 🏆 **1973**: Ajax
- 🏆 **1974**: Bayern Munich
- 🏆 **1975**: Bayern Munich
- 🏆 **1976**: Bayern Munich

- 🏆 **1977**: Liverpool
- 🏆 **1978**: Liverpool
- 🏆 **1979**: Nottingham Forest
- 🏆 **1980**: Nottingham Forest
- 🏆 **1981**: Liverpool
- 🏆 **1982**: Aston Villa
- 🏆 **1983**: Hamburg
- 🏆 **1984**: Liverpool
- 🏆 **1985**: Juventus
- 🏆 **1986**: Steaua Bucharest
- 🏆 **1987**: Porto
- 🏆 **1988**: PSV Eindhoven
- 🏆 **1989**: Milan
- 🏆 **1990**: Milan
- 🏆 **1991**: Red Star Belgrade
- 🏆 **1992**: Barcelona
- 🏆 **1993**: Marseille
- 🏆 **1994**: Milan
- 🏆 **1995**: Ajax
- 🏆 **1996**: Juventus

- 🏆 **1997**: Borussia Dortmund
- 🏆 **1998**: Real Madrid
- 🏆 **1999**: Manchester United
- 🏆 **2000**: Real Madrid
- 🏆 **2001**: Bayern Munich
- 🏆 **2002**: Real Madrid
- 🏆 **2003**: Milan
- 🏆 **2004**: Porto
- 🏆 **2005**: Liverpool
- 🏆 **2006**: Barcelona
- 🏆 **2007**: Milan
- 🏆 **2008**: Manchester United
- 🏆 **2009**: Barcelona
- 🏆 **2010**: Internazionale
- 🏆 **2011**: Barcelona
- 🏆 **2012**: Chelsea
- 🏆 **2013**: Bayern Munich
- 🏆 **2014**: Real Madrid
- 🏆 **2015**: Barcelona
- 🏆 **2016**: Real Madrid

MOST GOALS IN A TOURNAMENT

 **Cristiano Ronaldo—17** (Real Madrid, Spain—2015–16)

Cristiano Ronaldo—16 (Real Madrid, Spain—2013–14)

 Jose Altafini—14 (Milan, Italy—1962–63)

 Lionel Messi—14 (Barcelona, Spain—2011–12)

 Ferenc Puskas—12 (Real Madrid, Spain—1959–60)

 Gerd Müller—12 (Bayern Munich, Germany—1972–73)

 Ruud van Nistelrooy—12 (Manchester United, Netherlands—2002–03)

 Lionel Messi—12 (Barcelona, Spain—2010–11)

COPA LIBERTADORES

WINNERS

1960: Peñarol
1961: Peñarol
1962: Santos
1963: Santos
1964: Independiente
1965: Independiente
1966: Peñarol
1967: Racing
1968: Estudiantes
1969: Estudiantes
1970: Estudiantes
1971: Nacional
1972: Independiente
1973: Independiente
1974: Independiente
1975: Independiente
1976: Cruzeiro
1977: Boca Juniors
1978: Boca Juniors

1979: Olimpia
1980: Nacional
1981: Flamengo
1982: Peñarol
1983: Grêmio
1984: Independiente
1985: Argentinos Juniors
1986: River Plate
1987: Peñarol
1988: Nacional
1989: Atlético Nacional
1990: Olimpia
1991: Colo-Colo
1992: São Paulo
1993: São Paulo
1994: Vélez Sársfield
1995: Grêmio
1996: River Plate
1997: Cruzeiro
1998: Vasco da Gama

1999: Palmeiras
2000: Boca Juniors
2001: Boca Juniors
2002: Olimpia
2003: Boca Juniors
2004: Once Caldas
2005: São Paulo
2006: Internacional
2007: Boca Juniors
2008: LDU Quito
2009: Estudiantes
2010: Internacional
2011: Santos
2012: Corinthians
2013: Atlético Mineiro
2014: San Lorenzo
2015: River Plate
2016: Atlético Nacional

MOST GOALS IN A TOURNAMENT

 **Daniel Onega—17**
(River Plate, Argentina—1966)

Luizão—15
(Corinthians, Brazil—2000)

Norberto Raffo—14
(Racing, Argentina—1967)

Palhinha—13
(Cruzeiro, Brazil—1976)

Mário Jardel—12
(Grêmio, Brazil—1995)

MOST WINS BY COUNTRY:

 24 Argentina
 17 Brazil
 8 Uruguay
 3 Colombia
 3 Paraguay
 1 Chile
 1 Ecuador

MOST TOURNAMENT WINS

Independiente
(Argentina)—**7**

Boca Juniors
(Argentina)—**6**

Peñarol
(Uruguay)—**5**

Estudiantes
(Argentina)—**4**

GLOSSARY

Here are the meanings of some words relating to soccer rules, tactics, and equipment.

Added time
The amount of time added at the end of each half to make up for stoppages during the game.

Assist
A pass in a game that directly leads to a goal.

Attacking team
The team that is in possession of the ball.

Away game
A game that is played in the opponent's stadium.

Back four
The four players in front of the goalkeeper who form the defensive line.

Bench
The area next to the field in which the team staff and substitutes sit during a game.

Box-to-box midfielder
A midfielder who plays in both attack and defense, moving from one penalty box to the other.

Byline
The markings along the edge of the field between the goalposts and corner flags.

Caution
When the referee shows a player a yellow card for a serious offense.

Center circle
The circular marking in the middle of the field.

Center spot
The mark in the middle of the field, where the ball is placed during kick off.

Clean sheet
Describes a result in which a team does not concede a goal in a game.

Clearance
A defensive move in which a player kicks the ball away from goal.

Corner arc
The white arc at each corner of the field from which corners are taken.

Cross
A ball kicked from the side of the field, aimed at a teammate in or near the penalty area.

Far post
The goalpost furthest from where the ball is in play.

First touch
The first contact a player makes with the ball to control it.

Formation
The arrangement of the different players on a field—the formation dictates whether a team plays in an attacking or defensive style.

Goal kick
The method of restarting play when the ball has crossed the goal line when last touched by an attacking player.

Goal line
The line marking between the goal posts; a goal is awarded when the whole ball crosses the goal line.

Handball
An infringement in which a player (other than the goalkeeper) touches the ball with the hand or arm.

Halftime
The 15-minute rest period between the first and second halves.

Hat trick
Describes the feat of a player who scores three goals in a single game.

Injury time
The time added at the end of each half to make up for time lost to injuries, fouls, substitutions, and other incidents.

Kick off
The method of starting a game, or restarting play after a goal. Two teammates place the ball on the center spot and kick the ball into play.

Man marking
A method of defending set pieces in which each defender is responsible for watching a specific attacker.

Near post
The goalpost closest to where the ball is in play.

Offside trap
A move in which the back four step forward together in an attempt to put the opposition into an offside position.

Overtime
The two additional 15-minute periods played in cup tournaments when the score is still tied after 90 minutes.

Own goal
When a player scores against his own team, usually through an accidental deflection.

Penalty shootout
A method of deciding a winner when scores are still level after overtime.

Playmaker
A player, typically a midfielder, who controls the team's attacking flow.

Professional foul
A foul deliberately committed to stop the opponent from scoring.

Sending off
A situation in which the referee shows a red card to a player, who must leave the playing field immediately.

Set piece
Refers to the method—either a throw-in, corner, or free kick—used to restart play after an infringement or after the ball has gone out of play.

Substitution
The changing of players during the course of a game. In competitive matches, a team can make up to three substitutions.

Sweeper
An extra defensive player who helps the back four by dealing with any defensive errors.

Technical area
The area outside the touchline from which managers shout instructions to the team during a game.

Throw-in
The method of restarting play when the ball goes over the touchline. It involves throwing the ball back in play while keeping both feet on or outside the touchline.

Touchline
The marking along each side of the field that denotes the edge of the playing field.

Wall
The line-up of defenders during a direct free kick, who try to limit the shooting angle of the free-kick taker.

Zonal marking
A defensive system of play in which players are given a specific area to guard.

INDEX

Page numbers in **bold**
refer to main entries

ACKNOWLEDGMENTS

Dorling Kindersley would like to thank Carron Brown for the index, Anna Limerick for proofreading, and Nick McCabe for additional advice.

The publisher would like to thank the following for their kind permission to reproduce their photographs:

(Key: a-above; b-below/bottom; c-center; f-far; l-left; r-right; t-top)

1 Getty Images: Dmytro Aksonov (cb). 2 Dreamstime.com: Tom Wang (tr). Getty Images: Dmytro Aksonov (cr). 3 Alamy Stock Photo: Fredrick Kippe (tc). Getty Images: Dmytro Aksonov (cla); Dmytro Aksonov (bl); Dmytro Aksonov (c); Peter Read Miller / Contributor (tr). 4-5 Dreamstime.com: Tom Wang. 6-7 Dorling Kindersley: Stuart Jackson-Carter | SJC Illustration. 7 123RF.com: Konstantin Kalishko (tl). 8-9 Bridgeman Images: National Football Museum, Manchester, UK. 9 National Football Museum: (tr). 10 123RF.com: alhovik (tr); Richard Thomas (clb). Getty Images: Hulton Archive / Stringer (tl). 10-11 123RF.com: Andrey Kryuchkov (cb). 11 123RF.com: alhovik (clb/ball, crb/ball); Andriy Popov (crb). iStockphoto.com: 4x6 (clb). 12-13 Getty Images: Dmytro Aksonov. 14 Mary Evans Picture Library: Illustrated London News Ltd (tl). 14-15 Rex Shutterstock: Xinhua News Agency. 16 123RF.com: Gordana Damjanovic (clb); yukipon (cb); Christos Georghiou (crb). 18-19 Getty Images: Dmytro Aksonov. 20 Getty Images: Popperfoto (cr). iStockphoto.com: Arkhom1983 (cb). Mary Evans Picture Library: (bc). 20-21 Getty Images: David Price (b). 21 Getty Images: Imagno (ca); Popperfoto (cl, cb, bc). 22-23 KJA-Artists: Jon@KJA-Artists. 23 Pitch Heating Limited: (bc). 24 123RF.com: Olexandr Moroz / alexandrmoroz (cra). SWNS.com Ltd: (bl). 26-27 KJA-Artists: Jon@KJA-artists. 28-29 Nike: (c). 29 iStockphoto.com: richjem (tr). 30-31 KJA-Artists: Jon@KJA-artists. 30 Getty Images: Ian Kington (bc); Visionhaus (cla). 31 Getty Images: Dean Mouhtaropoulos (bc); Jean-Sebastien Evrard / AFP (c). 32-33 Getty Images: Dmytro Aksonov (background); Matthew Ashton (t). 34-35 123RF.com: Monika Mlynek (Stadium). Fotolia: Fotoedgaras

(Stopwatch). Getty Images: Bernhard Lang. 34 Getty Images: Helios de la Rubia (tl). iStockphoto.com: jamielawton (tc); PeopleImages (tr). 35 Getty Images: Gallo Images - Robbert Koene (tc); Alex Grimm / Bongarts (tr). Rex Shutterstock: Friedmann Vogel (tl). 36 Getty Images: Ben Radford (clb). 38-39 Getty Images: Dmytro Aksonov. 40-41 Rex Shutterstock: Image Source. 41 Rex Shutterstock: Matthew Impey / Wired Photos (crb). 42 Alamy Stock Photo: Reuters (clb). Dreamstime.com: Tungphoto (c). 44-45 Getty Images: Jamie Squire / Staff / Getty Images Sport. 46-47 Getty Images: Dmytro Aksonov / E+. 46 123RF.com: Ogm (bl). 48-49 Photo courtesy GoalControl GmbH. 49 Getty Images: Cameron Spencer / Staff (tr). 50 Catapult: (tl). Dorling Kindersley: Jon@KJA-Artists (tr). 54-55 Getty Images: Dmytro Aksonov. 56-57 Getty Images: Dmytro Aksonov. 57 Getty Images: Dmytro Aksonov (baclground). 58 Getty Images: Dmytro Aksonov (c). 58-59 Getty Images: Dmytro Aksonov. 59 Getty Images: Dani Pozo / Stringer / AFP (bc); Dmytro Aksonov (cr); Dmytro Aksonov (cl). 60 Getty Images: Jean-Yves Ruszniewski / Contributor (clb). 60-61 Getty Images: Dmytro Aksonov. 62-63 Getty Images: Dmytro Aksonov; Dmytro Aksonov (taking the kick). 63 Getty Images: Popperfoto / Contributor (bc). 64-65 Getty Images: Dmytro Aksonov (Background); Dmytro Aksonov (c). 64 Getty Images: Matthias Hangst / Staff (clb). 66-67 Getty Images: Dmytro Aksonov (Background); Dmytro Aksonov (c). 66 Getty Images: Pedro Ugarte / Staff / AFP (cl). 68-69 Getty Images: Dmytro Aksonov (Background); Dmytro Aksonov (b). 72-73 Alamy Stock Photo: Fredrick Kippe. 74-75 Getty Images: Dmytro Aksonov. 74 Getty Images: Drew Hallowell / Stringer (cl). 77 Getty Images: Ullstein Bild / Contributor (tr). 79 Getty Images: STF / Staff / AFP (br). 81 Press Association Images: (tr). 82-83 123RF.com: Monika Mlynek (background). 84 Getty Images: Rolls Press / Popperfoto / Contributor (bc). 84-85 123RF.com: Monika Mlynek. 88-89 123RF.com: Monika Mlynek. 90 Getty Images: Popperfoto / Contributor (tc); Popperfoto / Contributor (cla);

Mondadori Portfolio / Contributor (cra); Popperfoto / Contributor (br). 91 Dorling Kindersley: Adam Brackenbury / Stefan Podhorodecki (r). Getty Images: Matthew Ashton - AMA / Contributor (tl); Jasper Juinen / Staff (ca); Popperfoto / Contributor (clb); VI-Images / Contributor (bl); VI-Images / Contributor (cb). 93 Dreamstime.com: Connie Larsen (br). 94-95 Getty Images: Dmytro Aksonov. 98-99 KJA-Artists: Jon@KJA-Artists. 100-101 Allianz: (ca/all images). 102 Dreamstime.com: Dmitry Rukhlenko (cb). Getty Images: Gary Burchell (crb); Yosuke Tanaka / Aflo (l). 102-103 123RF.com: Andrey Kryuchkov (b). 103 Dreamstime.com: Berean (clb). Getty Images: Creative Crop / Digital Vision (cb); Yosuke Tanaka / Aflo (r). 104-105 Getty Images: Westend61. 104 Rex Shutterstock: Brad Smith / ISI / REX (br). 105 123RF.com: Burak Cakmak (br); Wavebreak Media Ltd (bc). Getty Images: Steve Bardens-FIFA / Contributor / FIFA (tr). Rex Shutterstock: John Dorton / ISI / REX (bl). 106-107 123RF.com: Videodoctor (c). 107 Getty Images: Marcus Brandt / Staff / AFP (br). 108 Getty Images: Stuart MacFarlane / Contributor (clb). 108-109 Dreamstime.com: Libux77 (c). Getty Images: Image Source (b). 110-111 Getty Images: Dmytro Aksonov. 111 Getty Images: Conor Molloy / Contributor (crb). 114-115 Getty Images: Peter Read Miller / Contributor. 116-117 Getty Images: Bob Thomas / Contributor. 116 Getty Images: Popperfoto / Contributor (tl). Rex Shutterstock: Colorsport / REX (cra). 118-119 Getty Images: Shaun Botterill / Staff. 119 Getty Images: Getty Images / Staff (tr); AFP / Stringer (crb); Professional Sport / Contributor (cr). 120-121 Getty Images: Hector Vivas / Stringer. 121 Getty Images: Tim Clary / Staff / AFP (crb); AFP / Getty Images / Staff (cr); Popperfoto / Contributor (tr). 122-123 Getty Images: Liewig Christian / Contributor / Corbis Sport. 123 Getty Images: Gallo Images / Stringer (crb); Mark Thompson / Staff (cr); Bob Thomas / Contributor (tr). 124 Alamy Stock Photo: Reuters (tl). Rex Shutterstock: Jurnasyanto Sukarno / EPA / REX (cl); Stringer / EPA / REX (clb). 124-125 Rex Shutterstock: Paul Miller / Epa /

REX. 126-127 Getty Images: Stuart Franklin - FIFA / Contributor / FIFA. 127 Getty Images: Al Bello / Staff (crb); Bob Thomas / Contributor (cr). TopFoto.co.uk: © 2003 Credit:Topham / PA (tr). 128-129 Getty Images: Christopher Morris / Contributor. 129 Getty Images: Tommy Cheng / Staff (tr); Paul Gilham / Staff (cr). Rex Shutterstock: Imago / Back Page Images / REX (crb). 130-131 Getty Images: Matthias Hangst / Staff. 130 Getty Images: VI-Images / Contributor (cl). Rex Shutterstock: Colorsport / REX (clb). TopFoto.co.uk: © PA Photos (tl). 132-133 Getty Images: Popperfoto / Contributor. 133 Getty Images: Vanderlei Almeida / Staff (cr); Jefferson Bernardes / Stringer (br); Sergio Goya / Stringer (tr). 134-135 Dreamstime.com: Donkeyru. 136-187 Dreamstime.com: Donkeyru. 138-139 Dreamstime.com: Donkeyru. 141 iStockphoto.com: Dmytro Aksonov (br)

Cover images: Front and Back: Dreamstime.com: Agencyby (Trophy icon), Burlesck (Football icon), Kirsty Pargeter (Background); Front: 123RF.com: Andres Rodriguez cr, Allan Swart c; Dreamstime.com: Michaelnivelet c/ (Net), Pixattitude cb; iStockphoto.com: Dmytro Aksonov fbr, peepo bl; Nike: br; Back: iStockphoto.com: Dmytro Aksonov r; KJA-Artists: Jon@KJA-artists bl; SWNS.com Ltd: cla; Spine: iStockphoto.com: Dmytro Aksonov t

All other images © Dorling Kindersley

For further information see: www.dkimages.com

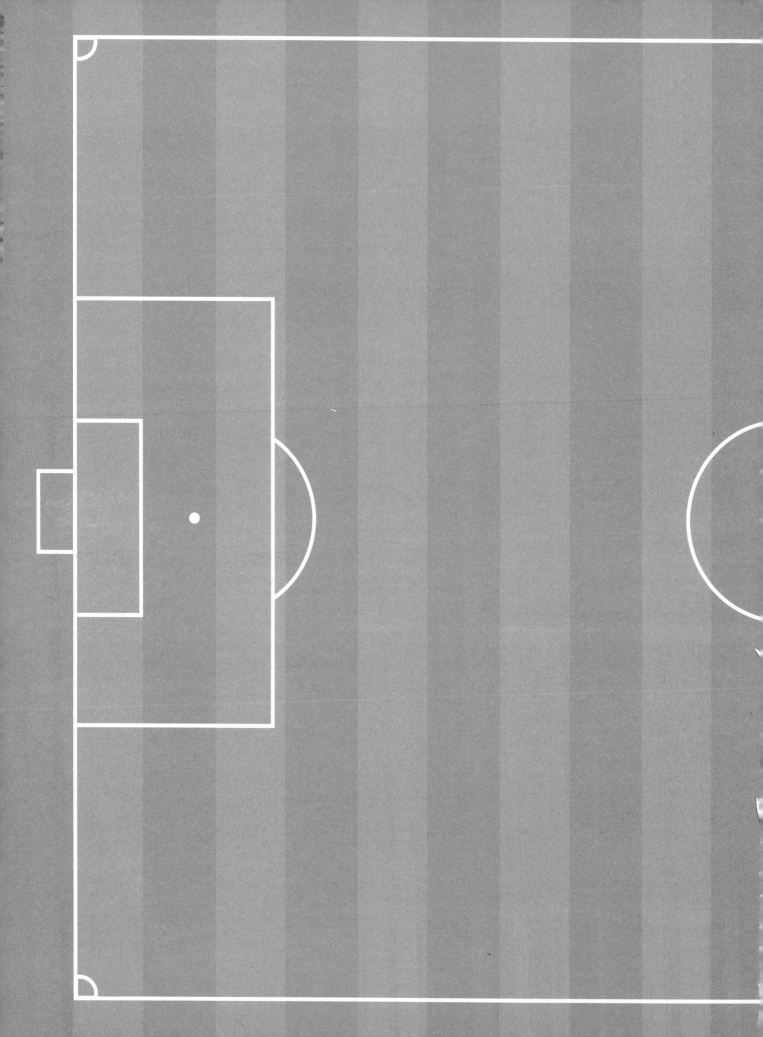